Massachusetts Avenue

G Street

F Street

E Street

D Street

C Street

Constitution Avenue

Pennsylvania Avenue

dison Drive

Postal Museum
Union Station

M

North Capitol Street

New Jersey Avenue

The Capitol

4th Street

3rd Street

Jefferson Drive

ir and Space

American
Indian

Maryland Avenue

Independence Avenue

I|1016138

M
L'Enfant
Plaza

SMITHSONIAN MUSEUMS

ON OR NEAR THE NATIONAL MALL

Anacostia Community Museum, National Zoological Park,
and Steven F. Udvar-Hazy Center
are located elsewhere in the Washington, DC, metropolitan area.

OFFICIAL GUIDE TO THE
SMITHSONIAN

FIFTH EDITION

Smithsonian
Books

WASHINGTON, DC

Library of Congress Cataloging-in-Publication Data

Names: Smithsonian Institution, author.
Title: Official guide to the Smithsonian.
Description: Fifth edition. | Washington : Smithsonian Books, 2021.
Identifiers: LCCN 2020030035 | ISBN 9781588346827 (trade paperback)
Subjects: LCSH: Smithsonian Institution--Guidebooks. | Washington
    (D.C.)--Guidebooks. | New York (N.Y.)--Guidebooks.
Classification: LCC Q11.S3 S664 2021 | DDC 917.5304/42--dc23
LC record available at https://lccn.loc.gov/2020030035

Printed in Singapore, not at government expense
25 24 23 22 21   1 2 3 4 5

Published by Smithsonian Books
Director: Carolyn Gleason
Senior Editor: Jaime Schwender
Assistant Editor: Julie Huggins

Editor: Joanna Reams
Designer: Leah Germann

The following are among the many individuals who provided invaluable assistance in the preparation of this edition: Adina McGee, Allison Peck, Amelia Meyer, Bethany Bentley, Cynthia Brown, Deane Madsen, Donna Tuggle, Douglas Remley, Elisa Hough, Erin Beasley, Erin Rushing, Frank Edwards, Frederica Aldelman, Fernanda Luppani, Jennifer Zoon, Jim Wood, Joyce Connolly, Juliana Olsson, Kristen Quarles, Laura Duff, Laura Harger, Lauren Kolodkin, Laurie Bohlk, Lisa Austin, Lisa Dunham, Marc Sklar, Marcia Baird Burris, Marilyn Scallan, Marshall Emery, Migs Grove, Myriam Springuel, Rebecca Robinson, Rhys Conlon, Richard Stamm, Samantha Barry, Stanley Hackadon, Tanya Thrasher, and Tyler Jump.

Photo Credits: Adrian James Testa, Alan Karchmer, Alex Jamison, Carl C. Hansen, Chip Clark, Colleen Dugan, Connor Mallon, Doc Dougherty, Donald E. Hurlbert, Eric Long, Ernest Amoroso, Gary Mulcahey, Jaclyn Nash, James Di Loreto, Jennifer Renteria, Jessie Cohen, Jim and Pam Jenkins, Jim Preston, Joseph Campbell, Kate D. Sherwood, Katherine Fogden, Leah Jones, Lucia R.M. Martino, Mackenzie Risher, Mark Avino, Matt Flynn, Mehgan Murphy, Miguel Montalvo, Neil Greentree, Paul Fetters, R.A. Whiteside, Robert Harrell, Roshan Patel, Skip Brown, and Walter Larrimore.

Cover: Smithsonian Castle and the Enid Haupt Garden. Photo by Jeff Tinsley.
Pumpkin by Yayoi Kusama, Hirshhorn Museum and Sculpture Garden. Courtesy the artist, Ota Fine Arts and Victoria Miro. © YAYOI KUSAMA.

Endsheets: Map of the National Mall by Amber Frid-Jimenez with special assistance from National Capital Planning Commission

CONTENTS

WELCOME
TO THE SMITHSONIAN!

Through our nineteen museums, National Zoo, and numerous research centers, the Smithsonian offers a wide variety of exciting, inspiring experiences for the whole family. Whether you're interested in art, science, history, or culture, you can find something here for everyone. Through exciting exhibitions, *Smithsonian* magazine, the Smithsonian Channel, books, blogs, affiliate museums, lectures, and tours, the Smithsonian connects Americans to their heritage.

For more than 170 years, the Smithsonian has remained true to its mission, "the increase and diffusion of knowledge," and today maintains scholarly contacts or conducts research in more than 140 countries worldwide. The Smithsonian is involved in pressing issues of the day in science, education, and concerns of national identity. It is a vast enterprise that encompasses—in addition to exhibition halls and art galleries—laboratories, observatories, field stations, scientific expeditions, classrooms, performing arts events, publications, affiliate museums, the world's largest traveling exhibition service, a cable television channel, numerous websites, and much more.

Through its creative staff and collections, the Smithsonian presents the astonishing record of American historical, cultural, and scientific achievement with a scope and depth no other institution in the world can match. The remarkable collections of the Smithsonian are the basis for research, exhibitions, and public programs in art, history, and science. The collections include more than 155 million artifacts, works of art, and scientific specimens. Among them are objects that speak to our nation's inquisitiveness, bold vision, creativity, empathy, and courage: the Space Shuttle *Discovery*, Marian Anderson's Easter Sunday performance outfit, Thomas Edison's light bulb, Margaret Hamilton's Apollo 11 code, the Wright flyer, Mitchelene BigMan's powwow dress, *Electronic Superhighway* by Nam June Paik, and Mohammad Ali's boxing gloves.

At home, your visit can continue. Go to si.edu to learn more about the museums, explore virtual exhibits, and see collections not currently on display. You can also digitally explore the Smithsonian's collections through Smithsonian Open Access, an online database comprising millions of 2D and 3D images of objects and artifacts that are free to download, share, and reuse. Explore these images at si.edu/openaccess.

Enjoy your visit. Please come back often!

PREVIOUS: You can enter the Castle on the south side, from Independence Avenue and the Enid A. Haupt Garden.

RIGHT: "Apollo 50: Go for the Moon," a special event held in July 2019 for the 50th anniversary of Apollo 11, recreated the launch of the spaceship and told the story of the first Moon landing through full-motion projection mapping artwork on the Washington Monument.

VISITING THE SMITHSONIAN
IN WASHINGTON, DC

Begin your visit at the Smithsonian Visitor Center in the Smithsonian Institution Building (the Castle) on the National Mall, 1000 Jefferson Drive SW–between 9th and 12th Streets SW, open daily, except December 25, from 8:30 a.m. to 5:30 p.m. The Smithsonian Institution is a complex of nineteen museums, the National Zoo, and numerous research facilities. Seventeen museums and the Zoo are located in the Washington, DC, area. The Cooper Hewitt, Smithsonian Design Museum and the National Museum of the American Indian, George Gustav Heye Center are in New York City. Here is some basic information to help you plan your Smithsonian visit.

OPPOSITE: Located along the north side of the Arts and Industries Building is the Kathrine Dulin Folger Rose Garden.

Metrorail: Smithsonian station

For information about the Smithsonian, call 202-633-1000 (voice/tape), e-mail us at info@si.edu, or visit si.edu.

ADMISSION

Admission is free to all Washington-area Smithsonian museums and the National Zoo, and the National Museum of the American Indian, George Gustav Heye Center in New York. The Cooper Hewitt, Smithsonian Design Museum in New York charges admission. Timed-entry passes may be required to visit any Smithsonian museum. Please check si.edu/visit for more information, or check the individual museum's website.

HOURS

Most Smithsonian museums are open daily, except December 25, from 10 a.m. to 5:30 p.m. (check museum listings in this guide). Extended summer hours are determined each year. The Anacostia Community Museum is open from 10 a.m. to 5 p.m. The Smithsonian American Art Museum and the National Portrait Gallery are open from 11:30 a.m. to 7 p.m. At the National Zoo, March-October, grounds are open from 8 a.m. to 7 p.m. and buildings from 10 a.m. to 6 p.m.; November–February, grounds are open from 8 a.m. to 5 p.m. and buildings from 10 a.m. to 4:30 p.m. Please check museum websites for the most up-to-date information as you plan your visit.

HOW TO GET THERE

We recommend using public transportation when visiting Washington's attractions. Metrorail, Washington's subway system, and Metrobus link the downtown area with nearby communities in Maryland and Virginia. To locate the Metrorail station nearest the museum you wish to visit, see the individual museum entries in this guide. For more information, call Metro at 202-637-7000 or visit the website, wmata.com.

The Smithsonian does not operate public parking facilities for museums. Limited restricted street parking is available on and around the National Mall; posted times are enforced. Some commercial parking can be found in the area. Limited parking is available at the National Zoo for a flat fee. Lots fill early during the spring and summer months.

SMITHSONIAN VISITOR CENTER

Open daily (except December 25) from 8:30 a.m. to 5:30 p.m. in the Castle, the Smithsonian Visitor Center makes a great gateway for your journey—here you can find a new, interactive way to plan a route through exhibitions; get a grasp of the scope and scale of the Smithsonian; see collection highlights from each Smithsonian museum; watch a panda cam; tour the Castle and marvel at 19th-century architecture; find out what's going on around the Smithsonian; and consult with in-house experts about what to see and do. For general Smithsonian information, visit si.edu/contacts or call 202-633-1000.

ACCESSIBILITY

For information on access to the Smithsonian for visitors with disabilities, see the website at si.edu/visit/visitorswithdisabilities.

ONLINE INFORMATION

A wealth of information about the Smithsonian and its resources is available online at si.edu.

PHOTOGRAPHY

Cameras and cell phones are permitted for personal use in most museums. Photography is permitted in permanent collection exhibitions but generally prohibited in special, temporary exhibitions. The use of flash attachments, monopods, tripods, and selfie sticks is prohibited in all buildings. Exceptions to these rules may occur in any exhibition or building. Ask at the information desk in the museum you are visiting for specific guidelines about photography.

SERVICE ANIMALS

Service animals are permitted in all Smithsonian museums and the National Zoo. Emotional support animals and pets are prohibited.

BELOW: Make the Smithsonian Visitor Center in the Castle your first stop. It opens at 8:30 a.m., earlier than the museums, so it's a great place to begin your visit.

SMOKING

Smoking is prohibited in all Smithsonian facilities, including the gardens.

DINING

Food service is available in the National Air and Space Museum on the National Mall and its Steven F. Udvar-Hazy Center in Chantilly, Virginia; the National Museum of African American History and Culture; the National Museum of American History; the National Museum of Natural History; the National Museum of the American Indian; the Hirshhorn Museum and Sculpture Garden; the National Portrait Gallery; the Smithsonian American Art Museum; and the National Museum of the American Indian, George Gustav Heye Center in New York. The Castle Café offers light fare daily. The Zoo has a variety of quick-service dining facilities.

SHOPPING

Most museums have stores carrying books, crafts, clothing, jewelry, reproductions, toys, and gifts that relate to the collections.

ABOVE: In the Smithsonian Castle, *The Smithsonian Institution: America's Treasure Chest* exhibition offers a tantalizing sample of the breadth and depth of the Smithsonian's vast collections.

LEFT: The Chinese Moongate in the Enid A. Haupt Garden is a great place to relax and enjoy nature.

THE NATIONAL MALL

A long, open, grassy stretch from the Capitol to the Washington Monument, the original National Mall was an important feature of Pierre L'Enfant's 1791 plan for the city of Washington. He envisioned it as a "vast esplanade" lined with grand residences. Before the Smithsonian Institution Building (the Castle) was built in the mid-19th century, however, the National Mall was used mainly for grazing and gardens. To the west, beyond the spot where the Washington Monument now stands, were tidal flats and marshes. After those areas were gradually filled, the National Mall was officially extended in the 20th century to the Lincoln Memorial.

In 1850, New York horticulturist Andrew Jackson Downing was commissioned to landscape the National Mall. But his design, which called for curving carriage drives amid a grove of American evergreens, was only partly realized. By 1900, the National Mall had deteriorated. Its eyesores

included a railroad station with sheds, tracks, and piles of coal. Two years later, work was begun to implement L'Enfant's early concept. Over the years, much of his vision became reality, with the National Mall now lined by rows of museum and government buildings.

On the National Mall today, people jog, fly kites, toss Frisbees, or just stroll. Near the Castle, children ride on an old-fashioned carousel. Most summers, the colorful Smithsonian Folklife Festival fills the National Mall for several weeks with traditional music and crafts. On the benches alongside the walkways, visitors can rest while deciding which Smithsonian museum to explore next.

BELOW: The National Mall has traditionally been the setting for large-scale events in the nation's capital.

ESPECIALLY FOR CHILDREN

THINGS TO SEE AND DO AT THE SMITHSONIAN

Before your visit, go to si.edu/visit/kids or call 202-633-1000 to learn about special events and offerings for children.

NATIONAL AIR AND SPACE MUSEUM

Both locations of the National Air and Space Museum (on the National Mall and at the Steven F. Udvar-Hazy Center in Chantilly, Virginia) offer a range of programs for families, children, and school groups. Story Time for young learners, interactive displays, hands-on activities, science demonstrations that spark curiosity, and special family-oriented days invite visitors to discover and explore the wonders of air and space. Check at the museum's Southwest Airlines Welcome Center in the Mall building or the John L. Plueger Family Welcome Center at the Udvar-Hazy Center and ask about activities scheduled for the day. Older children especially enjoy the flight simulator rides and spectacular films shown on the five-story-high screens in the Lockheed and Airbus IMAX® Theaters. Fees are charged for simulators and films.

NATIONAL MUSEUM OF NATURAL HISTORY

Even after a tour of the museum's best-known treasures, families and children have much, much more to do here.

- Hundreds of live butterflies flit from flower to flower, sip nectar, and roost inside the cocoon-like butterfly pavilion in *Butterflies + Plants: Partners in Evolution*. To purchase a ticket, visit naturalhistory.si.edu/exhibits/butterfly-pavilion or visit the pavilion box office.

- Next door at the *O. Orkin Insect Zoo*, children can crawl through a termite mound, hold insects, and watch as staff members feed the tarantulas several times a day.

- *Q?rius, The Coralyn W. Whitney Science Education Center,* is the museum's interactive space for visitors of all ages. It's a place for doing that's part lab, part collections vault, and part do-it-yourself workshop. Visitors can unleash their curiosity in real-world discussions with scientists and interactions with thousands of authentic objects—with surprising results! The museum's youngest visitors can head to the Loft, an area filled with picture books and games that also hosts activities where kids can examine butterfly wings under a microscope, find out the difference between an alligator and a crocodile, and build a human skeleton.

NATIONAL MUSEUM OF AMERICAN HISTORY

Young visitors can explore 300 years of history in one house in *Within These Walls*; see an enchanting 23-room dollhouse; go onboard a Chicago Transit Authority car; learn about Bud, the dog who went along on the first across-the-USA car trip and see the goggles he wore in "America on the Move"; and more.

ABOVE: Young visitors get hands-on experience exploring touchable collections in Q?rius, an educational activity space at the National Museum of Natural History.

- Spark!Lab engages and empowers families to participate in the invention process at the museum as well as nationally and internationally through its many outreach efforts. Hands-on invention activities are designed around family-friendly themes that connect to museum collections and change every four months, ensuring that Spark!Lab visitors have something new to explore each time they visit.

- Object Project presents familiar objects in a new light, exploring how people, innovations, and social change shaped life as we know it. Visitors can uncover the history of everyday things, from refrigerators and bicycles to ready-to-wear clothing and household conveniences. Encompassing almost 4,000 square feet, this display features some 300 objects, a "magic" bicyclist's scrapbook, and a special version of *The Price Is Right* and offers visitors the chance to try on clothing virtually. Plus there are objects to touch—and objects that "talk"!

- Wegmans Wonderplace invites curious kids, from babies to age six, to "cook" in a kitchen inspired by Julia Child's, plant and harvest pretend vegetables and run the farm stand, find the owls hiding in a miniature replica of the Smithsonian's Castle building, and captain a tugboat based on a model in the museum's collection. Here we nurture the motivation behind innovation—the sense of wonder that causes us to ask why—or why not.

To inquire about special activities and exhibitions, ask at the Welcome Center on the second floor or the information desk on the first floor; call 202-633-1000; or visit the museum's website at americanhistory.si.edu.

NATIONAL MUSEUM OF AFRICAN AMERICAN HISTORY AND CULTURE

The National Museum of African American History and Culture offers a range of engaging, educational experiences for children and their families. Programs are inspired by the objects and stories within the museum's collections while also being developmentally appropriate and meaningful for learners. Weekly programs including Cultural Cuddles (babies to 12 months of age) and Toddling Treasures (12 months to 36 months of age) invite children to bond, play, and discover with their favorite grown-ups. For children of all ages, STEM Days, offered throughout the year, highlight African American STEM contributions while inspiring young minds to get excited about science, technology, engineering, and math.

Other free programs include Family Days, gallery-based programs, and musical performances. All programming is grounded in anti-bias and anti-racist principles, including the understanding and development of each child's healthy racial identity, their joy in human diversity and inclusion, their sense of justice, and their capacity to act for their own and others' fair treatment. For more information and a full schedule, visit nmaahc.si.edu/events.

NATIONAL MUSEUM OF THE AMERICAN INDIAN

The National Museum of the American Indian in Washington, DC, and New York City offers engaging opportunities for families to expand their knowledge and appreciation of Native cultures and traditions throughout the Americas. Families can enhance their visits to the museum by participating in hands-on activities, attending specially-themed festivals throughout the year, taking a tour, or seeing a film. Throughout the year the museum offers a wide variety of festivals, craft demonstrations, and performances that feature Native cultural arts—music, dance, drama, literature, and storytelling—in indoor and outdoor program venues. Stop by the Welcome Desk to learn which programs will be available on the day of your visit.

The museum's two locations are home to individual and unique imagiNATIONS Activity Centers. Designed for children, the interactive, family-friendly spaces provide visitors of all ages with a multitude of distinctive learning experiences. Native peoples have always used the natural world around them to meet their needs, and today many of their innovations and inventions are part of daily life for millions worldwide. Visitors to the centers can explore some of these ingenious adaptations through a variety of hands-on activities. Please check the museum's online calendar for details.

BELOW: A child and parent participate in Cultural Cuddles, a weekly event organized by the National Museum of African American History and Culture's Early Childhood Education Initiative.

FREER AND SACKLER GALLERIES

The popular ImaginAsia family program, which includes inspirational art tours and workshops for making hands-on projects to take home, offers young visitors the chance to discover Asian art and culture. The museum also frequently hosts family festivals celebrating different cultural areas and provides activity guides. For more information and a full schedule, visit asia.si.edu/kids.

NATIONAL MUSEUM OF AFRICAN ART

The National Museum of African Art offers a range of family-friendly, children-centered programs throughout the week. Be it weekday or weekend, visitors of all ages can learn about Africa and explore African arts through special thematic tours, hands-on art-making workshops, take-home projects, special family days, and much more. At-home activities for K–12 audiences are also available on the museum's website. For more information and a full schedule, visit africa.si.edu/education.

HIRSHHORN MUSEUM AND SCULPTURE GARDEN

ARTLAB+ is a radically inclusive digital-media studio that provides teens ages 13–19 with free, after-school drop-in programs and gives them a safe space in which to learn and explore. Teens work with artist mentors to create works using audio engineering, video production, digital photography, graphic illustration, game design, 3D design, sculpture, and creative writing. Programming encourages participants to become critical thinkers and hone their technological skills. The curriculum is driven by the interests of the teens, who are given the freedom to direct their own learning experiences as well as access to the latest tech and a wide range of art materials.

NATIONAL POSTAL MUSEUM

With state-of-the-art interactive displays, inviting exhibit design, and activities geared to adults and children, the museum is designed for a family audience. Spend time in some of the museum's many audiovisual and interactive areas, including computer kiosks where you can create a digital stamp collection or have your picture taken to put on a stamp. Climb aboard a big-rig cab, a mud wagon, and a railway mail car. Discover the story of Owney, a stray dog who became the mascot for the Railway Mail Service. Check the museum's website for the current schedule of public programs and participate in a variety of hands-on activities and crafts.

NATIONAL PORTRAIT GALLERY

Family programs at the National Portrait Gallery combine art, history, and storytelling to explore how we see ourselves and others. Through creativity and play, young visitors can enjoy a new activity every day in the galleries or in the Education Center and the Explore! Space, which are located on the first floor of the museum. For more information about upcoming programs, please visit npg.si.edu or call 202-633-5385.

SMITHSONIAN AMERICAN ART MUSEUM AND RENWICK GALLERY

Kids of all ages will delight in finding artworks made from bottle caps, tin foil, or televisions throughout the Smithsonian American Art Museum and its Renwick Gallery. Other free programs include Family Festivals, artist demonstrations, and musical performances. Developing scientists can watch conservators treat art treasures in the Lunder Conservation Center, and future curators can browse more than 3,000 objects in the Luce

OPPOSTITE: On the National Mall near the Smithsonian Castle, the carousel is open year-round, weather permitting, for a nominal fee.

LEFT: James Jones, a traditional hoop dance artist, performs at the National Museum of the American Indian's Living Earth Festival.

Foundation Center for American Art. Look for upcoming programs on the museum's website at AmericanArt.si.edu/events.

In addition, the Luce Foundation Center offers a daily self-guided scavenger hunt and an informal sketching program. ASL and verbal-description tours for deaf and visually impaired visitors are available twice monthly, or by prior arrangement; the museum also offers Morning at the Museum, a sensory-friendly program for children, teenagers, and young adults with disabilities and their families. More information about accessible programming can be found on the museum's website.

ANACOSTIA COMMUNITY MUSEUM

BELOW: Visitors from babies to age six can engage in hands-on learning in Wegmans Wonderplace at the National Museum of American History.

OPPOSITE: Henry Dreyfuss (1904-1972) and James M. Conner (b. 1922). Camera, SX-70, 1972. Manufactured by Polaroid Corporation (USA). Metal, plastic, leather. Museum purchase through gift of Neil Sellin (1999-2-2-a). Cooper Hewitt, Smithsonian Design Museum.

Anacostia Community Museum features year-round virtual and/or onsite resources such as school tours, teacher training, student career days, family art workshops, and a series of urban gardening projects throughout the school year for secondary school youth and their families. Also available are opportunities accessible remotely and/or in-person, for volunteerism and internships for high school students to earn community service hours, as well as ongoing youth-centered public programs that involve storytelling, art workshops, performances, and films.

NATIONAL ZOO

The National Zoo is a favorite destination for children of all ages. The Zoo is a world leader in giant panda conservation, and visitors can see these charismatic bears as they eat, sleep, and play. At Elephant Trails, learn how the Zoo's Asian elephants are helping keepers and scientists better understand and save this critically endangered species. Watch keepers train the Zoo's gorillas and orangutans to participate in their daily care at the Great Ape House and Think Tank. Step into the immersive Amazonia exhibit to see titi monkeys, emperor tamarins, and hawk-headed parrots navigate the treetops of their rainforest habitat. At the Reptile Discovery Center, come face to face with a Komodo dragon—the world's largest lizard—and many other endangered reptiles and amphibians, including crocodiles, tortoises, and frogs. Animal encounters, keeper talks, and research demonstrations take place throughout the day. To view a schedule of these programs, visit the Zoo's website at nationalzoo.si.edu.

COOPER HEWITT, SMITHSONIAN DESIGN MUSEUM

The collections of the museum as well as design basics are introduced to young visitors through various intergenerational programs, including Drop in on Design workshops and design activities for ages five and up and an Imagination Playground, where children engage in visualization and creative play. The museum also hosts a Design Camp every summer for ages 6–13; participants take part in lively challenges and gallery explorations and experience the design process through sketching, building, and playing.

ABOUT THE SMITHSONIAN

For many people, the red sandstone building called the Castle symbolizes the Smithsonian Institution. But the Smithsonian is much more than that. It encompasses nineteen museums, the National Zoo, and numerous research facilities. Centered on the National Mall in Washington, DC, the Smithsonian has facilities in other parts of the nation's capital, a number of states, the Republic of Panama, Chile, Belize, Greenland, and Antarctica.

The Smithsonian Institution is the world's largest museum complex and research center, with collections in every area of human interest numbering more than 155 million items, ranging from a magnificent collection of ancient Chinese bronzes to the Hope Diamond, from portraits of US presidents to the Apollo lunar landing module to a 3.5-billion-year-old fossil. The scope is staggering. All of these objects help us understand the past, consider the present, and preserve history for future generations.

Only a small part of the Smithsonian's collections is on display in the museums at any one time, but we are putting more of our experts and

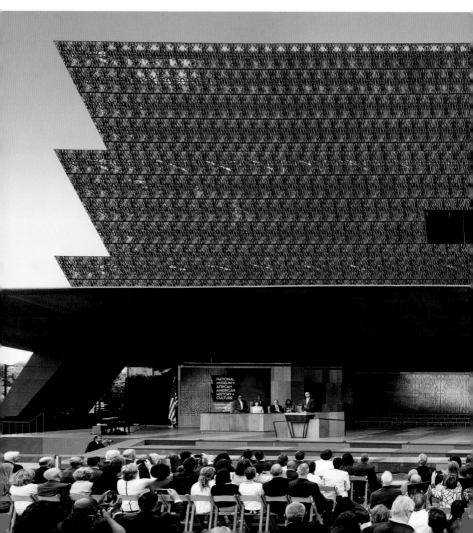

objects online. On expeditions to all parts of the world, Smithsonian researchers continually gather new facts and make discoveries in the fields of art, science, history, and culture.

HISTORY OF THE SMITHSONIAN

The Smithsonian owes its origin to James Smithson, a British scientist who never visited the United States. Smithson named his nephew, Henry James Hungerford, as the beneficiary in his will. He stipulated that should Hungerford die without heirs (as he did in 1835), the entire Smithson fortune bequeathed to Hungerford would go to the United States of America. The purpose would be to "found at Washington,

BELOW: President Barack Obama speaks at the dedication of the National Museum of African American History and Culture on September 24, 2016.

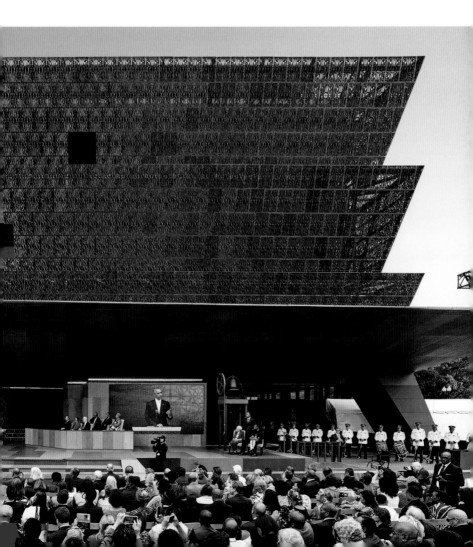

under the name of the Smithsonian Institution, an establishment for the increase and diffusion of knowledge."

On July 1, 1836, Congress accepted Smithson's legacy and pledged the faith of the United States to the charitable trust. In 1838, after British courts had approved the bequest, the nation received Smithson's estate—gold sovereign coins packed in leather bags, then the equivalent of more than a half-million dollars, a great fortune in those days. Eight years later, on August 10, 1846, President James K. Polk signed an act of Congress establishing the Smithsonian Institution in its present form and providing for the administration of the Smithson trust, independent of the government, by the Board of Regents of the Smithsonian and the secretary. With the formal creation of the Smithsonian came a commitment to the work that continues today in research, the operation of museums and libraries, and the dissemination of information in the fields of science, art, and history.

Today the Smithsonian is a national institution that receives a substantial appropriation from the federal government. Essential funding also comes from private sources, including the Smithson trust, other endowments, individuals, foundations, corporations, and revenues raised from such activities as membership programs, an online retail store, museum stores, and food services. The chief executive officer is the secretary. The Smithsonian is governed by the Board of Regents, which by law is composed of the vice president of the United States, the chief justice of the United States, three members of the Senate, three members of the House of Representatives, and nine private citizens. The chief justice has traditionally served as chancellor of the Smithsonian.

Each museum has its own director and staff. The central administration of the Smithsonian is headquartered in the Castle building.

LEFT: A statue of Joseph Henry, first secretary of the Smithsonian, enjoys a prominent setting at the Castle's entrance on the National Mall.

SMITHSONIAN SECRETARIES: 1846 TO TODAY

JOSEPH HENRY (1846–1878)★, a physical scientist and pioneer and inventor in electricity, was founding secretary. Henry set the Smithsonian's course with an emphasis on science.

Naturalist **SPENCER FULLERTON BAIRD** (1878–1887) developed the early Smithsonian museums and promoted the accumulation of natural history specimens and collections of all kinds.

SAMUEL PIERPONT LANGLEY (1887–1906), whose focus was aeronautics, astrophysics, and astronomy, launched the Smithsonian in those directions.

Under **CHARLES DOOLITTLE WALCOTT** (1907–1927), a geologist and paleontologist, the National Museum of Natural History and the Freer Gallery of Art opened, and the National Collection of Fine Arts (now the Smithsonian American Art Museum) became a separate museum.

CHARLES GREELEY ABBOT (1928–1944), a specialist in solar radiation and solar power, established a bureau to study the effects of light on plant and animal life.

During the tenure of ornithologist **ALEXANDER WETMORE** (1945–1952), the National Air Museum (now the National Air and Space Museum) and the Canal Biological Area (now the Smithsonian Tropical Research Institute) became part of the institution.

LEONARD CARMICHAEL (1953–1964), a physiological psychologist and former president of Tufts University, oversaw the opening of the National Museum of History and Technology (now the National Museum of American History).

Under the leadership of **S. DILLON RIPLEY** (1964–1984), a biologist, ecologist, and authority on birds of East Asia, the Smithsonian added the Hirshhorn Museum and Sculpture Garden, the National Museum of African Art, the Renwick Gallery, and the Cooper-Hewitt, National Design Museum (now the Cooper Hewitt, Smithsonian Design Museum).

ROBERT MC.C. ADAMS (1984–1994), an anthropologist, archaeologist, and former university administrator, placed new emphasis on broadening the involvement of diverse cultural communities and enhancing research support and educational outreach. The National Museum of the American Indian was established as part of the Smithsonian.

I. MICHAEL HEYMAN (1994–1999), a law professor and former chancellor of the University of California at Berkeley, guided the Smithsonian to reach out to Americans who do not visit Washington, DC. Initiatives included the first traveling exhibition of Smithsonian collections; a Smithsonian website; and the Affiliations program for the long-term loan of collections.

During the tenure of **LAWRENCE M. SMALL** (2000–2007), the Smithsonian opened the National Air and Space Museum's Steven F. Udvar-Hazy Center and the National Museum of the American Indian; reopened the renovated Donald W. Reynolds Center for American Art and Portraiture; and established the National Museum of African American History and Culture.

G. WAYNE CLOUGH (2008–2014) expanded the Smithsonian's global relevance and emphasized research, education, and scientific discovery. He made more of the collections accessible through a digitization effort and oversaw the opening of Sant Ocean Hall at the National Museum of Natural History and the reopening of the National Museum of American History.

DR. DAVID J. SKORTON (2015–2019), a board-certified cardiologist, was the first physician to lead the Smithsonian. During his tenure, the National Museum of African American History and Culture opened on the Mall.

LONNIE G. BUNCH III began his tenure in June 2019. He is increasing the institution's focus on education, especially for grades K–12, as well as greater inclusion and diversity in the research and history the Smithsonian highlights. An educator, historian, and author, Bunch was the founding director of the Smithsonian National Museum of African American History and Culture.

*Dates in parentheses signify years as secretary.

THE CASTLE

The Smithsonian Institution Building, popularly known as the Castle, was designed in medieval revival style (a 19th-century combination of late Romanesque and early Gothic motifs) by James Renwick Jr., architect of Grace Church and St. Patrick's Cathedral in New York and the Renwick Gallery of the Smithsonian American Art Museum in Washington.

A disastrous fire in 1865—just ten years after the Castle was completed—caused extensive damage and the loss of valuable objects. Restoration of the building took two years. In the 1880s, the Castle was enlarged and much of it remodeled.

The Castle originally housed the entire Smithsonian, which included a science museum, a lecture hall, an art gallery, research laboratories, administrative offices, and living quarters for the secretary and his family.

Today, administrative offices, the Smithsonian Visitor Center, and the exhibition *The Smithsonian Institution: America's Treasure Chest* are located here. The Smithsonian Visitor Center opens daily (except December 25) at 8:30 a.m. Here visitors can have their questions answered by volunteer information specialists and pick up free brochures on the Smithsonian.

BELOW: The Smithsonian Castle was designed by architect James Renwick Jr. and completed in 1855.

OPPOSITE: The Downing Urn in the Smithsonian's Enid A. Haupt Garden was originally erected on the National Mall in 1856 in memory of landscape designer Andrew Jackson Downing.

SMITHSONIAN GARDENS

Smithsonian Gardens has created several beautiful spaces around the Smithsonian museums on the National Mall. All have been designed to complement the museums they border and enhance the overall museum experience. Staff and docents lead weekly tours of some of the gardens from May through September (weather permitting). Visit any information desk for details.

The south side of the Mall features the Enid A. Haupt Garden, a 4¼-acre garden named for its philanthropic donor. An ornate parterre in the center is flanked by the Asian-inspired Moongate and Moorish Fountain Gardens. Other gardens on this side of the Mall include the Freer Gallery of Art's formal courtyard garden; the fragrant Kathrine Dulin Folger Rose Garden, next to the Castle; the colorful Mary Livingston Ripley Garden; and the Hirshhorn Museum and Sculpture Garden, where the plantings provide an ever-changing backdrop for the large-scale artworks on display outdoors. The native landscape at the National Museum of the American Indian and terraced beds at the National Air and Space Museum provide year-round interest for visitors.

On the Mall's north side, extensive landscape design at the National Museum of African American History and Culture includes a green roof, reading grove, pavilion with seating, and the Oculus, a water feature that also brings light into the museum's Contemplative Court. The Victory Garden at the National Museum of American History is typical of vegetable gardens planted during World War II, while the nearby outdoor exhibit, *Common Ground*, shares compelling stories about plants. The Pollinator Garden and the Urban Bird Habitat at the National Museum of Natural History spotlight plantings that provide food and shelter for migrating wildlife species.

Beneath the Haupt Garden is a three-level underground museum, research, and education complex that contains the Arthur M. Sackler Gallery, the National Museum of African Art, and the S. Dillon Ripley Center. The museums are accessible through aboveground entrance pavilions. Through a bronze-domed kiosk, visitors enter the Ripley Center, named for the Smithsonian's eighth secretary. It houses the International Gallery with its changing exhibitions, workshops and classrooms for public programs, and a lecture hall. The Smithsonian Associates and the Contributing Membership Program have their offices in the Ripley Center.

A CENTER FOR LEARNING

The Smithsonian is deeply involved in public education for people of all ages. Visiting groups of schoolchildren are common sights in the museums, and families come together here on weekend outings and summer vacations. Educators from the elementary school through the university level use the Smithsonian's resources, as do scholars pursuing advanced research. Through public classes, lectures, performances, and studio arts courses, the Smithsonian offers a wide range of lifelong learning opportunities. The Smithsonian also offers an exciting schedule of "living exhibits." Performing-arts activities include music, theater, dance, film programs, and Discovery Theater performances for children.

CENTER FOR FOLKLIFE AND CULTURAL HERITAGE

As one of the research units of the Smithsonian, the Center for Folklife and Cultural Heritage promotes greater understanding and sustainability of cultural heritage across the United States and around the world through its Smithsonian Folklife Festival, Smithsonian Folkways Recordings, Ralph Rinzler Folklife Archives and Collections, and Cultural Sustainability Program.

SMITHSONIAN FOLKLIFE FESTIVAL

Founded in 1967, the annual Smithsonian Folklife Festival promotes folk and traditional practices and honors the individuals and communities who sustain them. It provides a platform on the National Mall— "America's Front Yard"—for artisans, musicians, dancers, cooks, and others to share their creativity, heritage, and innovation with visitors from around the globe. One of five congressionally mandated national celebrations, the Folklife Festival has become an international model for research-based, community-engaged public programming.

LEFT: Nestled between the Arts and Industries Building and the Hirshhorn Museum and Sculpture Garden, the Mary Livingston Ripley Garden displays dozens of unusual varieties of plants in raised beds along a curvilinear brick path.

RIGHT: The Kathrine Dulin Folger Rose Garden showcases beautiful flowers and other vegetation that support healthy relationships between people, plants, and insects.

SMITHSONIAN LATINO CENTER

The Smithsonian Latino Center (SLC) ensures that Latino contributions to arts, history, national culture, and scientific achievement are explored, presented, celebrated, and preserved. The SLC empowers a greater understanding and deeper appreciation for the enduring contributions of Latinos to American history and culture. It preserves a growing collection of diverse stories and experiences and convenes conversations, inclusively, about the stories and connections that continue to inspire generations to come. In 2022, the SLC will open the Molina Family Latino Gallery at the National American History Museum, making the gallery the first museum space on the National Mall dedicated to celebrating the US Latino experience. Learn more at latino.si.edu.

SMITHSONIAN ASIAN PACIFIC AMERICAN CENTER

The Smithsonian Asian Pacific American Center (APAC) shares Asian Pacific American history, art, and culture through innovative museum experiences online and throughout the United States. Since 1997, APAC has created, coordinated, and partnered with hundreds of Asian Pacific American initiatives across the institution, ranging from collections, exhibits, cultural festivals, public programs, research, fellowships, and internships. Learn more at smithsonianapa.org.

RESEARCH AT THE SMITHSONIAN

The Smithsonian is a preeminent research center. Its research activities are known throughout the world for their benefit to the scholarly community and the advancement of knowledge. Smithsonian researchers explore topics as diverse as global environmental concerns, the nature of the world's changing human and social systems, and the care and preservation of museum objects.

SMITHSONIAN LIBRARIES AND ARCHIVES

The Smithsonian Libraries and Archives is a system of twenty-one branch libraries and an institutional archive that support the current work of the institution and researchers around the world while preserving the Smithsonian's past. Collections include 2.5 million library volumes encompassing a range of topics from art to zoology, and more than 44,000 cubic feet of archival records documenting the Smithsonian's history. All locations are open to the public, though advance notice may be required. Digital exhibitions, digitized collections, and collection information may be found online at library.si.edu and siarchives.si.edu. (For information about the Smithsonian Libraries Exhibition Gallery, see the entry on the National Museum of American History on page 96.)

ARCHIVES OF AMERICAN ART

The Archives of American Art is the world's preeminent and most widely used research center dedicated to collecting, preserving, and providing access to primary sources that document the history of the visual arts in the United States. Headquartered in Washington, DC, the archives also has a research center in New York City. For more information, call 202-633-7940 or visit its website at aaa.si.edu.

CLOCKWISE FROM LEFT: Images from Smithsonian Libraries and Archives include Conard and Jones Co., *1916 Floral Guide*, 1916; Owen Jones, *Examples of Chinese Ornament: Selected from Objects in the South Kensington Museum and Other Collections*, 1867; John F. C. Mullen, *Official Guide of the Centennial Exposition of the Ohio Valley and Central States: Cincinnati, O., U.S.A.* 1888. Smithsonian Libraries.

MUSEUM CONSERVATION INSTITUTE

The Museum Conservation Institute (MCI) is the center for specialized technical collections research and conservation for all Smithsonian museums and collections. MCI staff collaborate with and serve as a resource for in-depth studies of art, anthropological and historical objects, and natural history and biological materials, using the most advanced analytical techniques to illuminate their provenance, composition, and cultural context. MCI studies are also used to improve the Smithsonian's conservation and collections storage capabilities. Such studies require the latest instrumentation, analytical expertise, and knowledge of archaeology, art history, biology, chemistry, conservation, conservation science, geology, mechanical engineering, and interpretive abilities, all of which are available through MCI. MCI responds to the threats facing cultural heritage in multiple and complex ways; for example, by working with partners on highly successful training programs at the Iraqi Institute for the Conservation of Antiquities and Heritage to support the rescue and recovery of Iraqi and regional cultural heritage artifacts. For more information, call 301-238-1240 or visit MCI's website at si.edu/mci.

SMITHSONIAN CONSERVATION BIOLOGY INSTITUTE

The Smithsonian Conservation Biology Institute (SCBI) leads the Smithsonian's global effort to save species, better understand ecosystems, and train future generations of conservationists. More than 200 SCBI scientists and their partners in more than 30 countries create and share knowledge to aid in the survival and recovery of species and their habitats. Their research provides critical data for the management of populations in human care and valuable insights for the conservation and management of wild populations.

SMITHSONIAN MARINE STATION AT FORT PIERCE

This research facility of the National Museum of Natural History, located in Fort Pierce, Florida, serves as a field station that draws more than 100 top scientists and students each year. Research focuses on the marine biodiversity and ecosystems of the Indian River Lagoon and the nearshore waters of Florida's east central coast. The station has also teamed with community partners to create a marine science outreach center and public aquarium. For information, visit naturalhistory.si.edu/research/smithsonian-marine-station.

CENTER FOR ASTROPHYSICS | HARVARD & SMITHSONIAN

This research center is part of the Center for Astrophysics | Harvard & Smithsonian (CfA) in Cambridge, Massachusetts. CfA scientists are recognized leaders in theoretical astrophysics, gamma-ray astronomy, solar and stellar physics, extrasolar planets, the Milky Way and other galaxies, and the dynamics and evolution of the universe. CfA has observatories in Arizona, Hawaii, Chile, Greenland, and Antarctica. The largest field facility is the Fred Lawrence Whipple Observatory on Mount Hopkins near Tucson, Arizona. CfA also manages the control center for NASA's Chandra X-Ray Observatory. For information regarding public programs, visit cfa.harvard.edu or call the Public Affairs Office in Cambridge at 617-495-7461 or the Whipple Observatory at 520-879-4407.

SMITHSONIAN ENVIRONMENTAL RESEARCH CENTER

The Smithsonian Environmental Research Center (SERC) provides science-based knowledge to meet critical environmental challenges. SERC leads objective research on coastal ecosystems—where land meets the sea—to inform real-world decisions for wise policies, best business practices, and a sustainable planet. SERC's headquarters in Edgewater, Maryland, comprise 2,650 acres of diverse landscape and 16 miles of protected shoreline on the nation's largest estuary—Chesapeake Bay—25 miles east of Washington, DC. The site serves as a natural laboratory for long-term and cutting-edge ecological research. Here the Smithsonian explores the earth's most pressing environmental issues, including toxic chemicals, water quality, invasive species, land use, depleted fisheries, and global change. SERC also explains environmental science in innovative ways that transform how people view the biosphere and inspire them to take active roles in sustainable stewardship of the planet. SERC leads networks of research and education that extend across the coasts of the United States and around the world. For information, call 443-482-2200 or visit serc.si.edu.

BELOW: The 21-foot multiple mirror telescope glows against the sunset at the Center for Astrophysics | Harvard & Smithsonian's Fred Lawrence Whipple Observatory near Tuscon, Arizona.

LEFT: Ben Turner, staff scientist at the Smithsonian Tropical Research Institute in Panama, records soil characteristics in his field notebook.

OPPOSITE: Evan Keeling, graphic artist at Smithsonian Institution Exhibits, leads families in a Make Your Own Comic Book workshop during Smithsonian Week in Springfield, Massachusetts. The week of programming complemented the Springfield Museums' exhibition "Pop! Icons of American Culture from the Smithsonian," which featured 18 artifacts on loan from four Smithsonian museums.

SMITHSONIAN TROPICAL RESEARCH INSTITUTE

Headquartered in the Republic of Panama, the Smithsonian Tropical Research Institute is the world's premier tropical biology research organization, dedicated to increasing understanding of the past, present, and future of tropical biodiversity and its relevance to human welfare.

STRI's basic research is conducted primarily in tropical forest and coral reef ecosystems. STRI scientists discover new organisms, test scientific explanations for ecological adaptation and evolutionary innovation, develop methods to restore degraded lands, train students and teachers, and promote conservation of tropical ecosystems. STRI also coordinates the Center for Tropical Forest Science–Smithsonian Institution Global Earth Observatory (CTFS–ForestGEO), a global network of more than 60 forest research and monitoring stations on five continents. For information, visit stri.org.

SMITHSONIAN ACROSS AMERICA

The Smithsonian shares the depth and breadth of the institution's extraordinary collections and research with learners of all ages and educators everywhere. More than 300 educators and 200 affiliated organizations bring the Smithsonian's exhibitions and artifacts and inquiry-based lessons to more than 8 million learners across the globe each year. The Smithsonian's education programs offer a variety of traveling exhibits, educational workshops and programs, cultural presentations, and partnership opportunities, all of which can be tailored and combined to meet the needs of organizations and communities across America.

Visit www.si.edu/education to learn more about the offices working to achieve the Smithsonian's national outreach mission.

SMITHSONIAN AFFILIATIONS

Smithsonian Affiliations establishes and maintains the Smithsonian's long-term partnerships with museums, educational organizations, and cultural institutions in the United States, Puerto Rico, and Panama. Affiliates are partners on many of the Smithsonian's strategic priorities, adding content and expertise to national initiatives to amplify the power of the stories we tell and reach broader and more diverse audiences. Through Smithsonian Affiliations, millions of people have been able to experience the Smithsonian in their communities and have access to the Smithsonian's educational programs, inspiring exhibitions, and diverse collections. For more information regarding Smithsonian Affiliations or to find an affiliate near you, visit affiliations.si.edu.

SMITHSONIAN CENTER FOR LEARNING AND DIGITAL ACCESS

The Smithsonian Center for Learning and Digital Access produces and delivers Smithsonian educational experiences, services, and products informed by research and Smithsonian expertise and collections. Focusing on the needs of teachers and students, it collaborates with other educational organizations, especially to offer professional development. The center's website is an engaging digital destination for educators and learners of all abilities to discover, create, and share resources and ideas while developing knowledge and skills critical for academic and professional success. To explore this inspiring learning environment and to contact the center, visit learninglab.si.edu.

SMITHSONIAN INSTITUTION TRAVELING EXHIBITION SERVICE

The Smithsonian Institution Traveling Exhibition Service (SITES) has been sharing the wealth of Smithsonian collections and research programs with millions of people outside Washington, DC, for more than 65 years. SITES connects Americans to their shared cultural heritage through a wide range of exhibitions about art, science, and history. Exhibitions are shown not only in museums but also wherever people live, work, and play: in libraries, science centers, historical societies, community centers, botanical gardens, and schools. For exhibition descriptions and tour schedules visit sites.si.edu.

SMITHSONIAN SCIENCE EDUCATION CENTER

The Smithsonian Science Education Center (SSEC) develops science instructional materials for classrooms, builds awareness for science education among educational leaders, helps develop science education leadership for groups from school districts and states, and conducts programs that support the professional development of teachers. The SSEC was jointly established by the Smithsonian Institution and the National Academy of Sciences in 1985, and in 2010, the Smithsonian took on the full operation of the SSEC. Visit the center's website and learn more about the educational resources available at ssec.si.edu.

SMITHSONIAN ASSOCIATES

Established in 1965, Smithsonian Associates curates and produces informative, enlightening, entertaining, insightful programs to nurture and sustain a love of learning in audiences from pre-K to post-retirement. Inspired by and amplifying the full character of the Institution's research, collections, and exhibitions, Smithsonian Associates programs bring the Smithsonian to life!

Each year, Smithsonian Associates offers hundreds of lectures, courses, performances, hands-on studio art classes, and regional study tours to its members and the general public. Educationally focused Smithsonian Summer Camp, Discovery Theater, and Smithsonian Sleepovers foster the joys of learning for young people, their families, friends, and teachers from around the world.

In partnership with George Washington University's Corcoran School of the Arts and Design, a master of arts degree program in decorative arts and design history provides training for the next generation of curators, design specialists, and researchers.

For more information about the Smithsonian Associates programs or membership opportunities, call 202-633-3030 or visit SmithsonianAssociates.org.

OPPOSITE: "Men of Change: Power. Triumph. Truth." A traveling exhibition from the Smithsonian highlights revolutionary African American men whose journeys have altered the history and culture of the United States.

LEFT: Harvard professor and award-winning *Finding Your Roots* host Henry Louis Gates Jr. was among the distinguished guests sharing insights at a Smithsonian Associates program. Featured speakers and presenters at public programs also include museum curators, authors, scientists, historians, sports personalities, and cultural icons.

BELOW: Smithsonian Associates' Discovery Theater presents programs in Smithsonian museums and local schools. Featured here are actors portraying Jesse Owens and Wilma Rudolph.

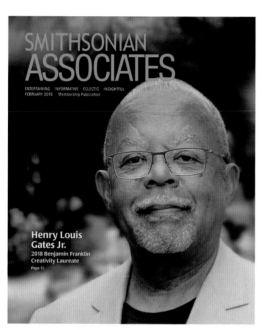

SMITHSONIAN
ASSOCIATES
ENTERTAINING   INFORMATIVE   ECLECTIC   INSIGHTFUL
FEBRUARY 2018   Membership Publication

Henry Louis
Gates Jr.
2018 Benjamin Franklin
Creativity Laureate
Page 11

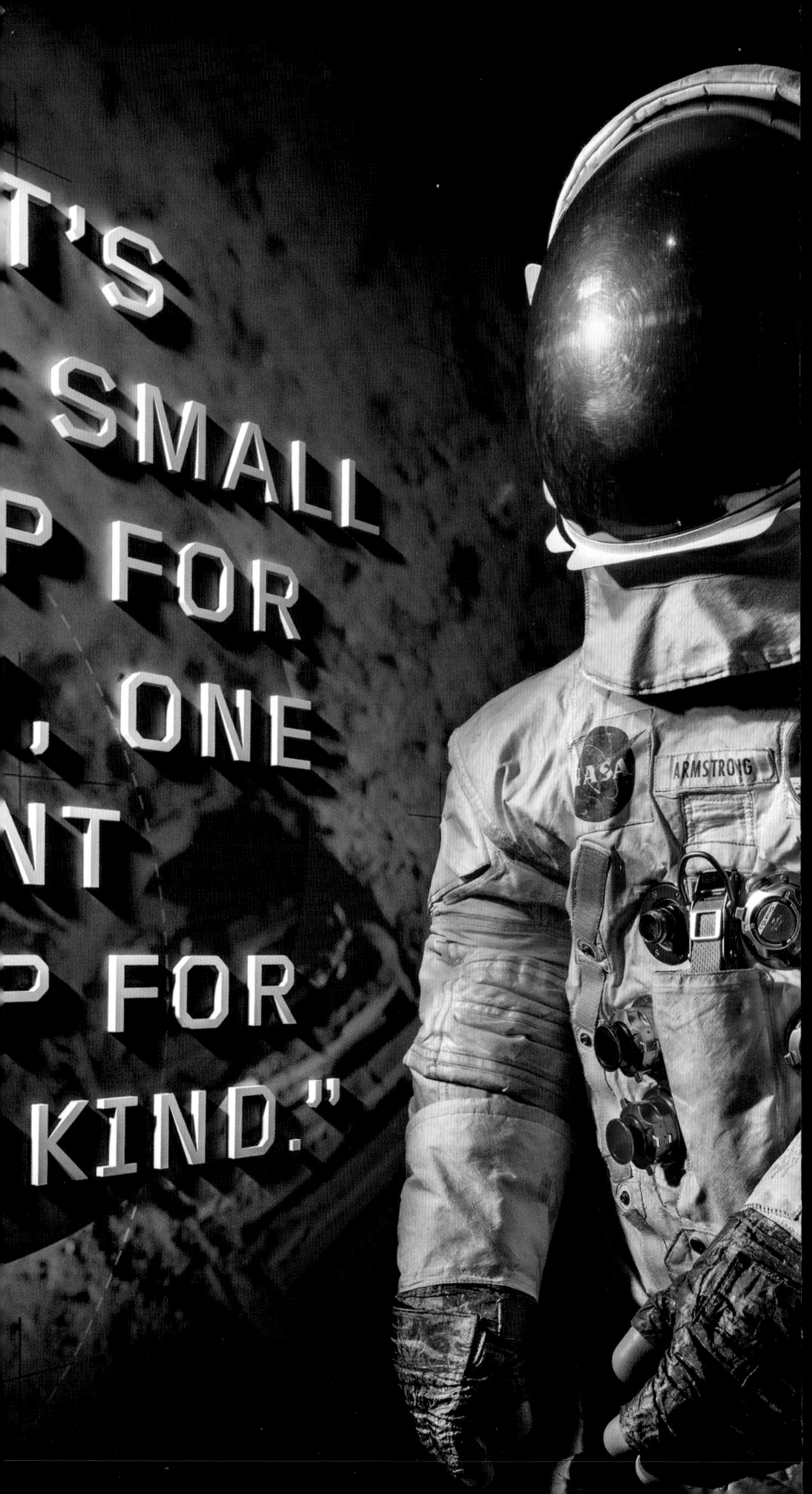
T'S
SMALL
P FOR
, ONE
NT
P FOR
KIND."
NASA
ARMSTRONG

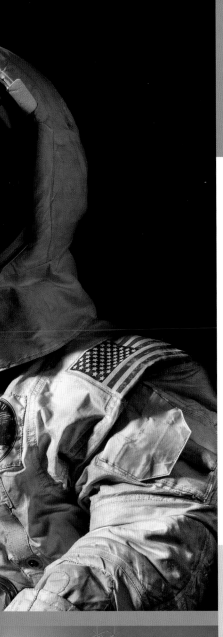

NATIONAL AIR AND SPACE MUSEUM

The 1903 Wright Flyer, Charles Lindbergh's *Spirit of St. Louis*, John Glenn's *Friendship 7*, Neil Armstrong's Apollo spacesuit, and the walk–through Skylab orbital workshop are just a few of the attractions in this vast and exciting museum. Not to be missed are guided tours and special IMAX® films projected on a screen five stories high and seven stories wide, providing a breathtaking cinematic experience.

OPPOSITE: The A7-L spacesuit worn by astronaut Neil Armstrong, commander of the Apollo 11 mission, when he first set foot on the Moon on July 20, 1969, still has visible gray lunar dust embedded in its surface.

IN WASHINGTON, DC
Jefferson Drive between Fourth and Seventh Streets SW. Open daily from 10 a.m. to 5:30 p.m. Closed December 25. Metrorail: L'Enfant Plaza station. Information: 202-633-2214

IN CHANTILLY, VA
Steven F. Udvar-Hazy Center, 14390 Air and Space Museum Parkway, off Route 28. Open daily from 10 a.m. to 5:30 p.m. Closed December 25. Parking available for a fee (parking fee is waived for vehicles entering after 4 p.m.).

Information: 703-572-4118
TTY: 202-357-1729
(for both museum locations)

airandspace.si.edu

Humanity achieved its eternal quest to reach the sky and soar in the heavens only in the most recent fraction of human history. This is one of the best places on Earth to see the amazing machines that made it possible and to learn the stories of the people who had ideas that defied expectations, convention, doubt, and setbacks to turn the impossible into reality. That's what makes the National Air and Space Museum the first stop for millions of visitors to Washington, DC, every year. Along with a close-up encounter with authentic artifacts of aviation and space, guests can enjoy large-screen IMAX® movies, flight simulators, guided tours, science demonstrations, and interactive devices.

The museum has two public display facilities. The museum in Washington, DC, showcases many one-of-a-kind artifacts, including the original 1903 Wright Flyer, Charles Lindbergh's *Spirit of St. Louis*, Neil Armstrong's Apollo 11 spacesuit (with lunar dust visible on the legs), John Glenn's *Friendship 7* spacecraft, and an Apollo lunar module. The Steven F. Udvar-Hazy Center in Chantilly, Virginia, exhibits thousands of artifacts, including a Lockheed SR-71 Blackbird, a Concorde, the Boeing B-29 Superfortress *Enola Gay,* and the Space Shuttle *Discovery* in an open, hangar-like setting. Within these two remarkable facilities—which constitute the largest complex in the world for presenting the history of air and space—visitors can marvel at the National Air and Space Museum's enormous, globally renowned collection.

Ongoing discoveries are also part of the museum's mission. Scientists in the Center for Earth and Planetary Studies conduct cutting-edge research, including work on NASA missions, and their expertise informs the museum's exhibits and programs. Museum historians continually bring new research and knowledge to telling stories of aviation and space innovation and exploration.

The Mall museum is open throughout a seven-year complete renovation that began in 2018. While many of its iconic air and spacecraft are always on display, there will be changes through 2025. When completed, all the galleries and public spaces will be transformed to inspire generations to come. For the latest information, visit airandspace.si.edu.

THE MUSEUM IN WASHINGTON, DC

The museum located in Washington, DC, presents the story of aeronautics and space flight in galleries devoted to a specific subject or theme. On display are historically significant aircraft, rockets, spacecraft, engines, scale models, spacesuits, awards, instruments, and pieces of flight equipment. Coming through the museum's entrance on the Mall, you're immediately surrounded by some of the most important airplanes, rockets, and spacecraft in history.

GALLERY 100. BOEING MILESTONES OF FLIGHT HALL

The first steps into the museum and the *Boeing Milestones of Flight Hall* immerse visitors in aviation and space firsts. Look right as you enter to see Mercury *Friendship 7*, the spacecraft that took John Glenn on the first orbital flight for a US astronaut. Next to it is Gemini IV, which opened its doors in orbit to let Ed White outside for the first US spacewalk. Another first nearby is the Viking Lander test vehicle, telling the story of the first spacecraft to successfully conduct science on the surface of Mars.

Just past the space capsules is an actual lunar module (LM2). Originally intended for a test

OPPOSITE: The National Air and Space Museum on the National Mall remains open while undergoing a complete renovation. Iconic air- and spacecraft remain on display throughout the project.

TOP: On June 3, 1965, Edward White became the first American to walk in space, after he floated out of the right hatch of this Gemini IV spacecraft. His commander was James McDivitt. They spent a total of four days in orbit.

flight, LM2 was used for ground testing instead. It is displayed as a highly accurate depiction of LM5 *Eagle*, which took Neil Armstrong and Buzz Aldrin to the Moon's surface on the Apollo 11 mission.

Want to touch a bit of the Moon yourself? The touchable Moon rock collected from the lunar surface by Apollo 17 astronauts sits across the hall near the Lockheed IMAX Theater. Towering to the left of the rock are the Pershing-II (US) and SS-20 (USSR) missiles, two disarmed missiles that represent the more than 2,600 nuclear intermediate-range ballistic missiles banned by the Intermediate Nuclear Forces Treaty of 1987. The US withdrew from the treaty in 2019.

Sometimes mistaken for a giant propeller, the massive NASA Full-Scale Wind Tunnel Fan hangs on the wall. Built in 1931 for the National Advisory Committee for Aeronautics, the predecessor to the National Aeronautics and Space Administration (NASA), the wind tunnel was used to test most of America's significant military aircraft of that era.

Of course, the museum's collection was meant to soar, so look up to see more firsts and record breakers, such as the bright orange Bell X-1 *Glamorous Glennis*, first to fly faster than the speed of sound and named for the wife of its pilot, Charles E. "Chuck" Yeager, who broke the sound barrier in 1947. Yeager, who fell off a horse shortly before the record flight, hid his broken ribs so he wouldn't be replaced on the record-setting flight.

Almost nose-to-nose with the X-1 is Charles Lindbergh's Ryan NYP *Spirit of St. Louis*, which he flew on the first solo nonstop transatlantic

flight in 1927. Because the plane was built without a front windshield (to make room for an extra fuel tank), Lindbergh had to look through a small periscope or out the side windows to orient himself. SpaceShipOne, high above the Viking Lander, won the Ansari X Prize in 2004 as the first privately developed, piloted vehicle to reach space.

The first jet engines that transformed flight are represented in the case below the Bell XP-59A Airacomet, which in 1942 became the first American turbojet aircraft. To keep its new technology secret, workers on the project added a fake propeller to the nose early in its development.

The first human-built objects to circle Earth are also represented. These include the backup for the first US satellite to orbit Earth, Explorer I, in 1958, and a replica of the first-ever artificial satellite to orbit Earth in 1957, the Soviet Sputnik 1.

With robotic spacecraft now soaring past the edge of the solar system, spacecraft such as Pioneer 10 and 11 highlighted in this gallery set humans on that path. The full-scale model in the museum was assembled from surplus equipment. Pioneer 10, launched in 1972, was the first robotic spacecraft to fly by Jupiter. Pioneer 11, launched in 1973, flew by both Jupiter and Saturn. A decade earlier, Mariner 2 was the first interplanetary probe to study another planet (Venus). The museum's engineering model was made from actual Mariner hardware.

OPPOSITE TOP: Flying his Ryan NYP *Spirit of St. Louis*, Charles Lindbergh became the first person to fly nonstop solo across the Atlantic, May 20–21, 1927. His flight between New York and Paris covered 3,610 miles in 33.5 hours.

OPPOSITE BELOW: Mariner 10 was the last launch in the Mariner series. The first probe to visit two planets, it launched on November 3, 1973, and reached Venus on February 5, 1974. Using the gravity from this planet like a slingshot, Mariner 10 first crossed the orbit of Mercury on March 29, 1974. The museum's Mariner 10 was a flight spare to the flown spacecraft.

BELOW: On October 14, 1947, while piloting his Bell X-1 *Glamorous Glennis*, US Air Force Capt. Charles E. "Chuck" Yeager became the first person to fly faster than the speed of sound.

GALLERY 109. HOW THINGS FLY

Massive machines soar through the sky to the Moon and beyond. How do they do that? Get the answers through interactive, hands-on experiences that explain to kids and adults alike the science behind the magic of flight and space exploration.

Understand the four basic forces of flight—gravity, lift, drag, and thrust—through interactive digital exhibits and feel their effects through mechanical exhibits that you operate. Hop in a Cessna 150 cockpit and see for yourself how pilots control a plane in flight. Other exhibits demonstrate supersonic speed, the structures and materials used in building air- and spacecraft, and more.

Learn from our amazing high school and college Explainers in their live demonstrations with fun experiments, unusual objects, and audience participation.

BELOW: The compact cockpit of the Bell X-1 featured an airspeed indicator at the top of the instrument panel. The Machmeter, which told Yeager when he had flown supersonically, is immediately to its right.

With all your new aerospace knowledge, head to the AAR Design Hangar. Take a design challenge focused on fun, creative projects that introduce the engineering design process. Participants can imagine, plan, build, and test prototypes.

After you leave, you can still enjoy *How Things Fly* through its website. Explore the physics of flight. Test fly an aircraft, build and launch a rocket, design your own paper airplane, learn how a jet engine works, or ask a Museum Explainer a question related to air or space at howthingsfly.si.edu.

GALLERY 110. GO FLY ZONE

Choose from a variety of ride simulators, including a sortie in vintage aircraft, and try to become a jet combat ace as you pilot the simulator into 360-degree barrel rolls. Select either pilot or gunner responsibilities. Take a virtual reality ride into space or take a group of friends on aviation- and space-themed trips in a dynamic motion simulator. These tickets are not timed; just get in line and take a ride. Fees apply.

GALLERY 111. EXPLORE THE UNIVERSE

Since humans first looked to the stars, they wanted to get closer and know what these amazing twinkling objects were. Take a stroll through the history of humanity's quest to see farther and more clearly into the universe. This gallery shows how new instruments reveal new universes. What do we know about where we are?

Start with early astronomical tools like astrolabes, quadrants, and a celestial globe dating from 1090 to the 1600s, together with reproductions of other instruments such as Galileo's early 1600s telescope. Then move on to the latest high-tech observatories on Earth and in space. See how these revolutionary instruments let people first see our place in the universe.

For many years, the answer to learning more was building larger, more precise, Earthbound telescopes (such as the 20-foot telescope used by William Herschel beginning in the 1700s) to study the structure and nature of the universe. See the tube and mirror from Herschel's famous telescope. Check out the observing cage and camera from the 100-inch telescope at Mount Wilson Observatory in Southern California. It was used by astronomer Edwin Hubble, whose discoveries in the early 20th century changed our understanding of the nature and motion of galaxies. Observe for yourself the prime focus spectrograph from the 200-inch telescope at

RIGHT: First launched from its White Knight mothership on August 7, 2003, the rocket-powered SpaceShipOne and its pilot ascended just beyond the atmosphere, arced through space (but not into orbit), then glided safely back to Earth.

LEFT: The backup primary mirror for the Hubble Space Telescope consists of two 1-inch glass disks fused to the faces of a thin, square eggcrate-like support structure. It was manufactured by the Eastman Kodak Company, and the blank for this mirror was fabricated by Corning Glass Works using their high-silicon Ultra Low Expansion Glass (ULE 7971).

Palomar Observatory in Southern California. The world's most sensitive camera mounted on the world's most powerful telescope, this instrument helped astronomers in the latter half of the 20th century study the most distant galaxies yet seen.

The Hubble Space Telescope took observations above the clouds and beyond the distortions of the atmosphere with a variety of sensing and image processing instruments. See the actual Hubble backup mirror, showing the honeycomb structure that supports the mirror surface. It's the backup to the one currently in use on Hubble.

The gallery also shares charge-coupled devices and other light detectors, the digital detectors from a variety of significant Earth-, air-, and space-based instruments that were designed to explore every facet of the universe.

GALLERY 113. MOVING BEYOND EARTH

Since November 2, 2000, there has been a continuous human presence in space aboard the International Space Station. What opportunities and challenges does human spaceflight offer? How do engineers make a reusable spacecraft like the space shuttle? How do astronauts spend their days on the International Space Station? What was life like on the space shuttle? What plans are there for the future of space transportation and exploration?

Your shuttle mission begins with a walk around the space shuttle mid-deck mockup, just like the one where astronauts lived and worked. See the flight suits worn by the first US woman astronaut, Sally Ride, and astronaut Guy Bluford, the first African American in space, during their shuttle missions, and examine the tools used to repair the Hubble Space Telescope.

Look at the intricate piping, valves, and thousands of components that made up the space shuttle's main engine, learn how the shuttle system worked, and examine the large-scale model of the space shuttle with the orbiter, external tank, solid rocket boosters, and mobile launch platform.

Try your skills as a mission flight director or space station designer and see how much you know about spaceflight in the interactive activities and quizzes. Then explore the Earth, Moon, and Mars in an immersive, interactive display at the Google Liquid Galaxy.

TOP: Skylab, the first US space station, was occupied by three crews between May 1973 and February 1974. Astronauts prepared and ate their meals at a galley table, using warmer trays to heat canned foods and a water gun to rehydrate dried foods.

BELOW: The Apollo-Soyuz Test Project was the first American-Soviet spaceflight, docking the last American Apollo spacecraft with the then-Soviet Soyuz spacecraft in 1975.

GALLERY 114. SPACE RACE

Space Hall contains the artifacts that reveal the complex history of the competition in space between the United States and the Soviet Union as a non-shooting battlefield in the Cold War.

The world's first long-range ballistic missile, the German V-2 rocket, is the ancestor to many of today's large rockets. View the harsh conditions under which the Nazis built the V-2. Some of these rockets, seized after World War II, helped the United States and the Soviet Union to advance their homegrown technology. Visitors can see the how rocket technology progressed with examples like the US Navy's Viking sounding rocket, developed for scientific purposes (1949–1955), and Aerobee 150, which carried scientific instruments for probing the upper atmosphere (1955–1970).

Don't miss the one remaining piece of Sputnik, the first human-built satellite to orbit Earth, and the Jupiter-C and Vanguard rockets,

which the United States used to launch its answers to Sputnik in 1958. The US Air Force Minuteman III, an intercontinental ballistic missile, was a primary component of the US nuclear arsenal, and it remains so.

Of course, sending objects into space was only a first step. Next came animals and then people. Cosmonaut Yuri Gagarin became the first human to orbit the Earth, on April 12, 1961. Gagarin's training flight suit is on display.

Learn how cosmonaut Alexei Leonov became the first human to "walk" in space, in March 1965, by seeing the backups of his suit and airlock. Marvel at an Apollo 15 lunar suit that astronaut David Scott wore on the Moon in 1971 and compare it to the Soviet lunar Krechet spacesuit.

The Cold War also took to space in less famous ways, such as the Corona camera, which observed the Soviet Union from space from 1960 to 1972. Because this camera used film, it had to return from space and be recovered and its film developed to see what it had captured. The United States and USSR also spied on each other's communications throughout the Cold War, often from space.

After NASA's Apollo missions reached the Moon, US attention turned to long-term space dwelling. Walk through the Skylab Orbital Workshop, a backup for the first US space station, 1973–1974, to see the astronauts' abundant living space. (Don't forget to look up!) Easing tensions between the United States and the Soviet Union made cooperation possible on orbits and led to the first international space mission in 1975: the Apollo-Soyuz Test Project.

Throughout the Space Race, the United States continued peaceful scientific study of space, seeing farther into the universe than ever before. The museum's full-size engineering model of the Hubble Space Telescope was used for structural testing for the observatory that was put into orbit by the space shuttle in 1990. Next to it are Hubble components that astronauts returned following on-orbit repairs.

LOCKHEED MARTIN IMAX® THEATER

Large-format films are shown on a screen five stories high and seven stories wide. An admission fee is charged. Schedules are available at the theater box office or the Southwest Airlines Welcome Center. Accessible accommodations are available.

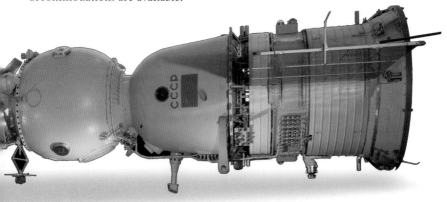

GALLERY 209. THE WRIGHT BROTHERS & THE INVENTION OF THE AERIAL AGE

It took less than 66 years from the Wright brothers' first successful flight until Neil Armstrong set foot on the Moon, and you can witness keys to those achievements in this gallery.

See the 1903 Wright Flyer, the first heavier-than-air, powered aircraft to make a sustained, controlled flight with a pilot aboard.

Learn the story of how Wilbur and Orville Wright reached that historic day in Kitty Hawk, North Carolina, when they first flew. Here you find a St. Clair bicycle, one of only five bicycles known to exist today that were manufactured by the cycle-making brothers. See a copy of the letter to the Smithsonian that Wilbur Wright wrote in 1899, asking for information about aeronautics.

Look at the tools they used, some of which they made themselves, to repeatedly test and learn, such as the wind tunnel instrument. There's also a reproduction of the lift balance with which the Wrights performed their pioneering wind-tunnel research, and the stopwatch they used to time their first flights.

Use hands-on mechanisms to test and learn about wing warping and other inventions made by the Wright brothers.

TOP: The original 1903 Wright Flyer, the world's first successful airplane, was built and flown by Wilbur and Orville Wright.

BELOW: The Apollo Lunar Module was a two-stage vehicle designed to ferry two astronauts from lunar orbit to the lunar surface and back. The lunar module-2 (LM-2), shown here, was used in testing. It has been modified to appear like the Apollo 11 lunar module *Eagle* that landed on the Moon in 1969.

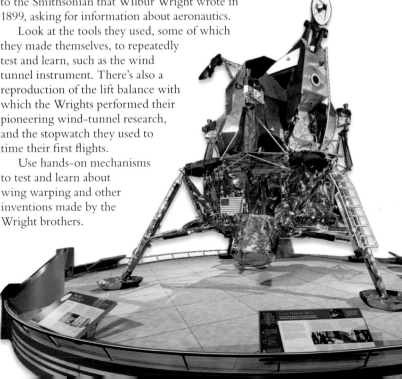

Watch video reenactments of the first four flights of the 1903 Wright Flyer on the First Flight simulations.

The Wright Flyer suffered damage after its first flights, but while certain parts were replaced, the gallery has some of the original fabric and a propeller. Both were on the Wright Flyer when it flew at Kitty Hawk in 1903.

A tiny piece of fabric and wood from the 1903 Flyer are on the wall of the gallery, framed after Neil Armstrong took them to the Moon on Apollo 11. Turn around from the frame to see Armstrong's Apollo 11 spacesuit. Note the gray, particularly below the knees, where this carefully conserved suit still has Moon dust embedded in its fabric.

GALLERY 213. TIME AND NAVIGATION

Once, humans sailed by the tides, Sun, and stars. Now satellites high above offer positional information with mapping precision that early explorers would envy. The key to it all is time, and here you can learn how revolutions in timekeeping over three centuries have influenced the way we find our way.

See how you would have done as a seafarer, using stars and interactive sextants to help plot your course. Discover how the Ramsden dividing engine ultimately led to mass production of precision octants and sextants. And check out how Apollo astronauts used an advanced version of this classic technology, the Apollo sextant and eyepiece, to stay on course to the Moon.

Before GPS and radar, Wiley Post flew his Lockheed Vega *Winnie Mae* around the globe twice in the 1930s. See how he accomplished this breakthrough in air navigation. And see how even with no connection to outside information, a ship can navigate using its inertial navigation system, as long as the instrument knows where it has started.

Sometimes a person isn't even needed to get a machine where it needs to be, like the Volkswagen Touareg Stanley, a car that in 2005 won the DARPA (Defense Advanced Research Projects Agency) Grand Challenge of having a vehicle navigate a complex course without a human driver.

Learn about other tricks and techniques for reaching a destination, like the way the Mariner 10 spacecraft (the museum's is a flight-qualified spare) used a gravitational assist from Venus to fly by Mercury three times in 1974 and 1975.

RIGHT: Record-setting aviator Wiley Post flew his Lockheed 5C Vega *Winnie Mae* around the world in 1931 and 1933. In 1935 he flew into the stratosphere while wearing the world's first pressure suit, which he helped design.

STEVEN F. UDVAR-HAZY CENTER

When your artifacts can fly themselves in, it helps to have a location adjoining a major airport. That is what the National Air and Space Museum's location in Chantilly, Virginia, offers—along with an unparalleled museum experience. Planes, spacecraft, and other artifacts are displayed in a massive open setting and organized by themes including commercial flight and military aircraft.

The 10-story Boeing Aviation Hangar uses all the space from floor to ceiling, with aircraft suspended on two levels from the building's huge trusses, and larger aircraft on the floor. The suspended vehicles replicate their typical flight maneuvers: a small two-seater flies level, an aerobatic airplane hot-dogs upside down, and a WWII fighter angles for a victory. Walkways rising four stories above the floor provide nose-to-nose views of aircraft suspended in flight.

The James S. McDonnell Space Hangar is dominated by the dramatically lit Space Shuttle *Discovery*, around which hundreds of other space artifacts are arranged. A free-floating simulated astronaut appears to be performing a spacewalk above, and oddly shaped satellites and sleek rockets dot the overhead space. The hangar features three elevated overlooks that allow visitors to study suspended artifacts up close and get a view of the entire hangar.

Around the corner on the walkways are overlooks of the Mary Baker Engen Restoration Hangar, where visitors can watch the museum's staff and volunteers conserve and restore amazing artifacts to preserve history and ensure that future generations can view them in wonder. Restoration work may not be active on weekends.

Ride up 164 feet to the Donald D. Engen Observation Tower, which gives visitors a great place to observe aircraft taking off and landing at the adjacent Washington Dulles International Airport.

Take in an amazing movie on the giant screen in the Airbus IMAX® Theater, or try your hand as fighter ace or space explorer in one of the simulators. Fees apply for both.

Outside the Udvar-Hazy Center, the Wall of Honor leads from the parking lot to the building's entrance. Panels are engraved with the names of those who have contributed to the nation's heritage in aviation and space exploration. A polished steel sculpture by John Safer, reaching 70 feet in the air, anchors the Wall of Honor. You can add the name of a loved one to the Wall and support the museum by visiting https://airandspace.si.edu/support/wall-honor.

THE BOEING AVIATION HANGAR

PRE-1920 AVIATION

A trip back to the days of fabric and wood aircraft is found near the entrance to the Boeing Aviation Hangar. These early birds include America's first fighter airplane, the Nieuport 28, a French design flown by US pilots in World War I. Nearby is the twin-engine Caudron G.4, used for reconnaissance, as a bomber, and in training. The museum's is one of only two that still exist.

Perhaps the most famous WWI aircraft—and definitely among the most significant—is the Sopwith Camel. Camels downed 1,294 enemy aircraft, more than any other Allied fighter in World War I.

COMMERCIAL AVIATION

As you explore the southern end of the Boeing Aviation Hangar, you'll see the big birds that mark key milestones in the commercial travel that billions now enjoy each year. They include the shiny silver Boeing 307 Stratoliner—the first airliner to have a pressurized fuselage, which allowed it to fly higher and provide a smoother trip for passengers. The museum's *Clipper Flying Cloud*, flown by Pan American Airways, is the only surviving Stratoliner. Speed and luxury drew the jet set to the Concorde SST, the first supersonic airliner to enter scheduled service. The museum's

BELOW: The World War II area of the Boeing Aviation Hangar includes important aircraft including an F6F Hellcat (top), P-38 Lightning (bottom center), and the world's first atomic bomber, the B-29 Superfortress *Enola Gay* (center).

OPPOSITE TOP: The Spad XVI was a two-seat version of the very successful single-seat Spad fighters of World War I, the Spad VII and the Spad XIII.

OPPOSITE MIDDLE: Based on the B-17C bomber, the Boeing 307 Stratoliner was the world's first pressurized airliner, flying comfortably "above the weather" for Pan American and TWA after it entered service in 1940.

OPPOSITE BELOW: In 1976, the Anglo-French Concorde became the first supersonic transport to enter scheduled service. Flying for Air France, the museum's Concorde opened the first SST service between Paris and New York, Washington, and Rio de Janeiro. The Concorde was retired in 2003.

Concorde was the first in the Air France fleet. The Boeing 367-80 (707 prototype), known as the Dash 80, was the original prototype for the Boeing 707, America's first jetliner and the airplane that opened the world to faster, less expensive air travel.

AEROBATIC FLIGHT

Continue past the pre-1920 craft, and you'll be in a land of loops, rolls, and spins with aerobatic craft above and on the floor around the Boeing 367-80. Leo Loudenslager accomplished the unprecedented by winning seven US National Aerobatic Championship titles in his red and white Loudenslager Laser 200 between 1975 and 1982, plus the 1980 World Champion title. On the way in, you may have passed under Betty Skelton's Pitts Special S-1C *Little Stinker*. She used it to win the International Feminine Aerobatic Championships in 1949 and 1950.

BUSINESS AVIATION

Surrounding the supersonic Concorde are stars from the history of business aviation, from the workhorse Beechcraft King Air, introduced in 1964 and still the world's most popular turboprop business aircraft, to the Learjet 23, the founding model of the original Lear Jet Corporation.

GENERAL AVIATION

Across the hangar are the aircraft that thousands across the nation use to pilot themselves for work and pleasure, including the classic Piper J-3 Cub. Thousands of private pilots, including many in the Civilian Pilot Training Program before World War II, trained in this easy-to-fly, inexpensive airplane. In 1964, Jerrie Mock became the first woman to pilot an aircraft around the world, flying the Cessna 180 *Spirit of Columbus*.

SPORT AVIATION

Around and above the Boeing 307 are sport aircraft like the Arlington Sisu 1A. It was the first motorless aircraft to fly beyond 620 miles during a single flight in 1964. John Monnett designed his Monnett Moni motor glider in the early 1980s. It could zip along at 120 mph or glide around in search of thermal updrafts.

ULTRALIGHT AIRCRAFT

Along the same side, near the nose of the Concorde, are craft that, while light and small, have given people new ways to explore and learn in the skies, like the Cosmos Phase II. A conservation group called Operation Migration, dedicated to replenishing the number of endangered birds, used this ultralight two-seater to lead flocks along new migration routes from Canada to the United States. One of the first twin-engine ultralights was the Ultraflight Lazair SS EC. This configuration marked an important step in increasing the reliability of these simple and inexpensive aircraft.

VERTICAL FLIGHT

At this end of the hangar, it's time to go straight up with helicopters and their relatives like the Autogiro Company of America AC-35. In 1935 this "roadable" gyroplane was a model for a suburban commuter aircraft. With folding blades and a powered drive wheel, it could do 25 mph on city streets and 90 mph in the air. The first presidential helicopter was a Bell H-13J in 1957.

ABOVE: The Moni (pronounced Moe-nee) is a kitplane motorized glider powered by a tiny engine originally developed for ultralight aircraft. John Monnett designed the Moni and sold kits to build it from 1982 to 1986.

BELOW: On July 12, 1957, President Dwight D. Eisenhower became the first sitting US president to travel by helicopter in this blue and white Bell H-13J. The Air Force acquired two H-13Js for the White House to evacuate the president in case of nuclear attack by the Soviet Union.

OPPOSITE: This French WWI airplane, the Caudron G.4, was used as a bomber, a reconnaissance aircraft, and a trainer. This example is one of only two that survive and is one of oldest multiengine airplanes in the world.

Its primary role was to evacuate the president in case of nuclear attack. Mixing the small landing and takeoff footprint of a helicopter with the speed and range of an airplane, the Bell XV-15 Tilt Rotor Research Aircraft took to the skies for the first time in 1977. It was one of NASA's most successful research aircraft, having performed two-and-a-half decades of experimental service.

LIGHTER-THAN-AIR FLIGHT

Near the Concorde's tail, you'll find lighter-than-air craft including the Goodyear Pilgrim blimp control car, the first modern Goodyear blimp. Records setters such as the Double Eagle II, the first balloon to fly the Atlantic, the Breitling Orbiter 3, the first balloon to fly nonstop around the world, and the Red Bull Stratos Gondola, which set world records for altitude and the highest parachute jump, are also found here.

SMALL ARTIFACTS

Along the wall nearby are hundreds of artifacts and collections, including aerial cameras, awards and insignias, machine guns, aircraft models, popular culture items, and pilot uniforms displayed in glass cases.

INTERWAR AND WWII MILITARY AVIATION

Making your way back toward the SR-71 Blackbird, you'll see planes from between the world wars and those that flew in World War II. Spreading its wings over much of the exhibit is the Boeing B-29 Superfortress *Enola Gay*. On August 6, 1945, the *Enola Gay* dropped the first atomic bomb used in combat on Hiroshima, Japan. The Boeing P-26A Peashooter, from between the wars, introduced the concept of the high-performance, all-metal monoplane fighter design, which was a radical departure from wood-and-fabric biplanes. Amphibious planes were common in the interwar period, like the Loening OA-1A *San Francisco* amphibian. It flew on the historic Pan-American Goodwill Flight of 1926 and 1927 through Mexico and Central and South America.

Aircraft from the United States, Germany, and Japan that did battle in the skies over Europe and the Pacific are all around. They include the Curtiss P-40E Warhawk, which wore a shark-mouth paint scheme and was one of the best-known US fighters of World War II. Its greatest fame was with the Flying Tigers. Germany's Arado Ar 234 B-2 Blitz (Lightning) was the world's first operational jet bomber and reconnaissance aircraft.

The Vought F4U-1D Corsair fighter-bomber, with its distinctive bent wing, earned a distinguished combat record in World War II and Korea. To help combat Japan's best fighters, the United States developed the Grumman F6F-3 Hellcat. Introduced in 1943, it gave American pilots an aircraft that was faster and almost as maneuverable as those used by the Japanese. With its unique twin booms, the twin-engine Lockheed P-38J Lightning was one of the most versatile fighters of World War II.

Among the most unusual WWII aircraft was the Aichi M6A1 Seiran (Clear Sky Storm). The museum's is the only surviving example of this Japanese bomber, which was designed to operate from submarines. Another breakthrough was pioneering a practical helicopter. Igor I. Sikorsky's efforts led to the Vought-Sikorsky XR-4C (1942)—the prototype for the world's first mass-produced helicopter.

COLD WAR AVIATION

Holding a place of honor, where you can stand back and admire its still futuristic design decades after it retired, is the Lockheed SR-71 Blackbird. On its final flight in 1990, this Blackbird set a transcontinental speed record by flying from the West Coast to the East Coast in 67 minutes and 54 seconds. Across from the Blackbird are other Cold War aircraft, including the McDonnell Douglas F-4S Phantom II, one of the most

versatile military aircraft ever built and flown by the US Air Force, Marine Corps, and Navy.

KOREA AND VIETNAM

Craft used in battle in Korea and Vietnam are close by, among them the North American F-86A Sabre. Above Korea, American pilots flying the Sabre established a significant victory ratio over enemy MiG-15s like the one next to the Sabre. Able to hit supersonic speeds, the Republic F-105 Thunderchief was designed as a single-seat fighter-bomber capable of carrying nuclear weapons or heavy bomb loads.

The first operational jet fighter to fly faster than the speed of sound in level flight was the North American F-100 Super Sabre. The model on display was flown by famous combat pilot Robbie Risner and also flew during the 1968 Tet Offensive.

Iconic for both its look and the unmistakable whop-whop-whop of its main rotor blade, the Bell UH-1H Iroquois "Huey" is what many think of when it comes to aviation during the Vietnam War. What the jeep was to Americans in World War II, the Huey was to those who fought in Vietnam.

MODERN MILITARY AVIATION

Coming up to the present, on display is the Lockheed Martin X-35B Joint Strike Fighter, a stealthy, multirole fighter currently in production. This aircraft was the first to achieve a short takeoff, level supersonic dash, and vertical landing in a single flight. The Mikoyan-Gurevich MiG-21F-13 Fishbed-C, which entered service in 1960, was the Soviet Union's first truly modern second-generation jet fighter. *Top Gun* fans will enjoy the Grumman F-14D(R) Tomcat, which was a mainstay of the US Navy for decades. The supersonic, twin-engine, two-place strike fighter gave legendary service to the Navy and was featured in the 1986 film starring Tom Cruise.

One of the museum's latest acquisitions is here as well. The Grumman EA-6B Prowler is a four-seat, twin-engine electronic-warfare plane that served for four decades from Vietnam up to 2019, when the museum's aircraft, the last one to be retired, flew in and went on display.

LEFT: The F-4 entered service with the US Navy in 1960 and soon became the premier fighter-bomber for the US Navy, Marine Corps, and Air Force, as well as with eleven other countries. The Museum's F-4 shot down a MiG-21 over Vietnam in 1972 as a Navy F-4J before being upgraded to an F-4S and ending its career with a Marine squadron.

AIRCRAFT ENGINES

A collection of aircraft engines is on display at ground level at the northeast end of the museum.

THE JAMES S. MCDONNELL SPACE HANGAR

ROCKETS AND MISSILES

Stroll past the tail of the SR-71 and enter the world beyond our Earthly home in the James S. McDonnell Space Hangar. See the Goddard 1940/41 P-Series rocket, one in a pioneering series that Robert Goddard, credited with creating the first liquid-fueled rocket, launched near Roswell, New Mexico, as he continued to develop his invention. The P-Series were the largest rockets tested there before Goddard moved to Annapolis, Maryland, in 1942 to undertake wartime work for the US Navy.

Descendants of Goddard's invention are all around, such as the Corporal missile—the first nuclear-armed ballistic missile deployed by the US Army—and NASA's Redstone missile. A modified version of the US Army's Redstone ballistic missile was used to send America's first astronaut, Alan Shepard, into space in 1961.

The Pegasus is a three-stage rocket used by commercial, government, and international customers to deploy small satellites into low Earth orbit, and the Agena-B Upper-Stage Launch Vehicle is part of the rockets used from 1959 until the mid-1980s as orbital injection vehicles or intermediate stage boosters for space probes.

SPACECRAFT AND SPACEWARE

The centerpiece of the hangar is the workhorse Space Shuttle *Discovery*. The longest-serving orbiter, *Discovery* flew 39 times from 1984 to 2011—more missions than any other spacecraft—spending altogether 365 days in space.

Among *Discovery*'s spacefaring predecessors is Gemini VII, which helped pave the way to the Moon. Astronauts Frank Borman and James A. Lovell Jr. were launched into orbit aboard this spacecraft on December 4, 1965. As the target of the world's first orbital rendezvous, it demonstrated that humans could survive in microgravity for at least two weeks. Later, the Manned Maneuvering Unit, a backpack propulsion device, gave astronauts untethered mobility for extravehicular activities outside the space shuttle.

Testing was also done without inconveniencing humans with the NASA Android. This articulated dummy, used in the development of spacesuits,

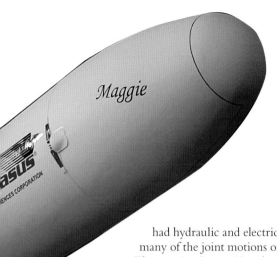

LEFT: Made to launch satellites into Earth's orbit, the Pegasus Launch Vehicle was first used in 1990 and has since launched dozens of satellites. Shown here is Pegasus XL, a version of the first US air-launched orbital launch vehicle developed by Orbital Sciences Corporation.

had hydraulic and electrical actuators that replicated many of the joint motions of the human body.

The massive Saturn V rocket entirely controlled itself through the launch and up to the separation of the Command and Service Module and Lunar Module. Its Saturn V instrument unit housed the guidance system for the Saturn V launch vehicle, which sent astronauts on their way to a lunar rendezvous.

ROBOTIC SPACE EXPLORATION

Even after going to space ourselves, we continue to send probes such as the Mars Pathfinder to explore where humans cannot—at least not yet. Museum visitors can see a test model of the spacecraft that landed on the Red Planet in July 1997, resting on its deflated protective airbags from its bouncing-ball landing. The Vega probe displayed is an engineering model of the Soviet spacecraft that flew by Venus in June 1985 and launched scientific instruments into the planet's atmosphere.

If you're okay with spiders, check out "Anita," a spider flown on Skylab for web formation experiments. Or if you wonder how the immense mirrors in telescopes are made, look at the Ritchey mirror grinding machine from the 1890s. This device demonstrated how extremely large telescope mirrors could be fabricated.

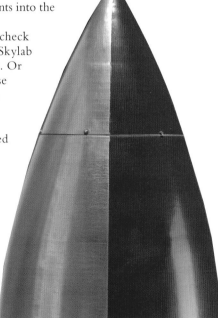

RIGHT: Robert Goddard, who invented the world's first liquid-propellant rocket in 1926, attempted to fly this A-series rocket in September 1935. After the failed launch, aviator Charles Lindbergh and philanthropist Harry Guggenheim asked Goddard to give a rocket to the Smithsonian.

APPLICATIONS SATELLITES

The remarkable uses of space gear included the Corona "bucket." This film-return capsule, recovered on May 25, 1972, from the last Corona photoreconnaissance satellite mission, brought back photos of the Soviet Union and other countries taken from space. The Applications Technology Satellite 1 was the first of a series of six satellites sponsored by NASA for research in the new field of space communications. The Sirius FM-4 satellite has provided more than 150 digital music and audio channels to North America since 2001.

These satellite wonders would not exist but for the computer, the massively parallel processor, and its expansion unit. While they may look like big plain boxes, together these three technologies revolutionized the processing of vast amounts of remote sensing data from space. They did this by allowing computers to perform operations on large amounts of data at the same time (in parallel).

SMALL ARTIFACTS

More than 500 small artifacts used in space, including cameras and personal gear, sounding rocket payloads, space-themed toys, and even borscht in tubes (prepared for Soviet cosmonauts), are exhibited in cases throughout the hangar.

BEHIND THE SCENES

The Udvar-Hazy Center also features the Mary Baker Engen Restoration Hangar, where visitors can watch museum specialists working on aircraft and spacecraft from a mezzanine overlook; the Archives Department, which is open to researchers; the Emil Buehler Conservation Laboratory; the Collections Processing Unit; and a collections storage area.

RIGHT: This articulated dummy was built for NASA's Manned Spacecraft Center by the Illinois Institute of Technology to support the development of spacesuits. It uses hydraulic and electrical actuators to replicate many of the joint motions of the human body.

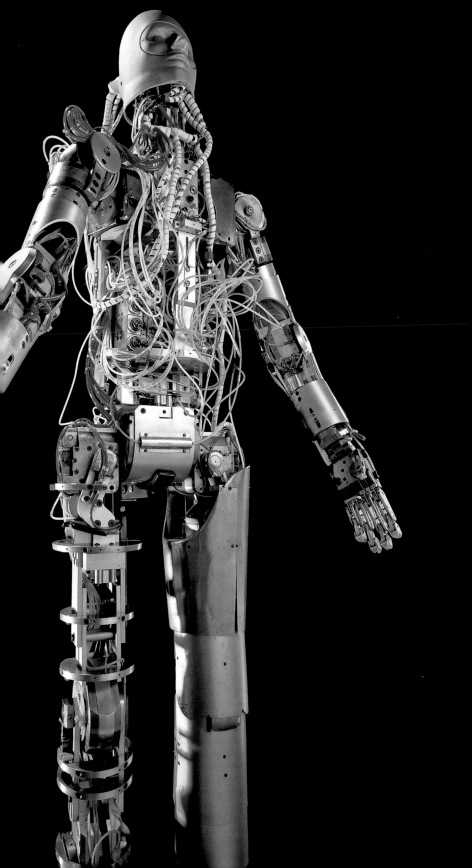

GENERAL INFORMATION

LOCATIONS
The National Mall building is on Jefferson Drive SW between Fourth and Seventh Streets SW in Washington, DC. Entrance: Jefferson Drive

The Steven F. Udvar-Hazy Center is near Washington Dulles International Airport at 14390 Air and Space Museum Parkway, Chantilly, Virginia. Entrance: off Route 28.

HOURS
Open daily from 10 a.m. to 5:30 p.m. Closed December 25.

GETTING THERE
Public transportation: The closest Metrorail stop to the National Mall building is the L'Enfant Plaza station. To get to the Udvar-Hazy Center, take the Metro Silver Line from L'Enfant (or other Silver Line stations) to the Wiehle-Reston East Metro station and transfer to the Fairfax Connector's 983 bus. Buses operate during museum hours. Fares and schedules can be found at fairfaxconnector.com or by calling 703-877-5965.

By car: The National Mall building does not have public parking, but many commercial parking lots are available in the area. Limited on-street parking includes some handicapped spaces. At the Udvar-Hazy Center, parking is available for a daily fee (parking fee is waived for vehicles entering after 4 p.m.)

VISITOR SERVICES
For information on the museum in Washington, DC, call 202-633-2214. For the Udvar-Hazy Center, call 703-572-4118. Send queries by e-mail to NASM-VisitorServices@si.edu or visit the museum's website, airandspace.si.edu.

TOURS
Highlights tours are given by museum docents daily at 10:30 a.m. and 1 p.m. at both locations. Groups can reserve guided tours (subject to safety and health guidelines). To reserve a tour, visit www.airandspace.si.edu/group-reservations, phone 202-633-2563, or for questions e-mail NASMTours@si.edu.

Schools: School-group reservations for tours, programs, and science demonstrations must be made in writing at least three weeks in advance. Details are available at airandspace.si.edu. For reservations, use the online form at https://airandspace.si.edu/visit/group-reservations, call Monday through Friday 202-633-2563 (voice/tape), or e-mail nasmtours@si.edu.

DINING
In the National Mall building: A café featuring grab-and-go sandwiches, salads, and snacks, along with hot dogs, pulled pork sandwiches, and soup, is on the first floor, just past the Space Race gallery. Food options are subject to change as renovations are completed at the building on the Mall. At the Udvar-Hazy Center: A restaurant is available with indoor seating. For full menu and details on additional food available, visit the museum web site airandspacemuseum.si.edu.

SHOPPING
The museum stores are on the second floor on the east end of the National Mall building and on the entrance level at the Udvar-Hazy Center. Museum store locations are subject to change as renovations are completed at the building on the Mall.

THEATERS
Large-format films are presented on giant screens in IMAX® theaters at both locations. For show information or to purchase tickets, visit www.si.edu/imax, or call 202-633-4629 or 866-868-7774.

ACCESSIBILITY INFORMATION
Both locations have access ramps and elevators. All theaters are wheelchair accessible, and most shows offer audio descriptions and/or closed caption reflectors. Wheelchairs (regular and bariatric) are available at both locations free of charge. The Aira app can connect visitors with sighted agents who provide visual descriptions of what is in front of visitors on demand (use of the app is free with in the Museum and connected to our wifi; details at www.Aira.io/faq). Tours

for persons who have visual, hearing, or other impairments may be arranged at least three weeks in advance by calling 202-633-2563.

WHAT'S UP
For monthly updates on museum events, subscribe to the National Air and Space Museum's e-newsletter, *What's Up*, at airandspace.si.edu/WhatsUp.

MEMBERSHIP
To become a member of the museum's National Air and Space Society and enjoy *Air & Space* magazine and other exciting benefits, call (202) 633-2603 or visit airandspace.si.edu.

ABOVE: P-26A Peashooter represented the state of the art in high-performance, all-metal monoplane fighter design in the mid-1930s. Its bright yellow wings aided rescuers in finding it if forced down. The distinctive black-and-white unit markings represent the 34th Attack Squadron of the US Army Air Corps.

OPPOSITE: The Corsair was introduced in combat in 1943. Because of design problems in early models that made it difficult to land aboard carriers, the Corsair became primarily known as a Marine Corps fighter, though it did serve on carriers as a fighter-bomber by the end of the war. The "bent-wing bird" was also used extensively during the Korean War in the ground attack role.

201
MILLION

TO

145
MILLION
YEARS AGO

145
MILLION

TO

66
MILLION
YEARS AGO

GIANT SHADOWS ON THE LANDSCAPE

NATIONAL MUSEUM OF NATURAL HISTORY

Dinosaurs, the Hope Diamond, the African bull elephant, and the huge North Atlantic right whale are among the most popular exhibits at the National Museum of Natural History. Also of special interest is Q?rius, an interactive learning space where visitors can explore thousands of authentic museum specimens and objects.

OPPOSITE: Encounter astonishing fossils in the *David H. Koch Hall of Fossils—Deep Time* exhibition as you explore your connection to all life on Earth.

Constitution Avenue entrance: 10th Street NW

Mall entrance: Madison Drive between 9th and 12th Streets NW

Open daily (except December 25) from 10 a.m. to 5:30 p.m. Extended hours posted on the museum website

Metrorail: Smithsonian and Federal Triangle stations (Orange/Silver/Blue lines) and Archives-Navy Memorial-Penn Quarter station (Yellow/Green line)

Smithsonian information: 202-633-1000, TTY: 202-357-1729

naturalhistory.si.edu

The National Museum of Natural History is dedicated to understanding the natural world and our place in it. As the nation's largest research museum, it is a treasure trove of more than 147 million natural and cultural objects. This encyclopedic collection serves as an essential resource for scientists studying earth sciences, the biological world, and human origins and cultures. Exhibitions and educational programs attract nearly 5 million visitors a year to the museum's green-domed Beaux-Arts building, one of Washington's best-known landmarks.

Only a tiny portion of the vast collections is on public display. Many of the objects are housed in the Smithsonian's Museum Support Center in Suitland, Maryland, a state-of-the-art facility for storage and conservation of research collections.

Behind the scenes in the laboratories and offices at the museum and the support center, more than 500 scientists conduct research in association with colleagues from universities, other museums, and government agencies.

The story told in the museum's exhibition halls—through displays, interactive carts, and our dynamic volunteers—is the story of our planet, from its fiery beginnings to its transformation over billions of years by a marvelous web of evolving life, including our own species. Living and nonliving, art and artifact—taken together, they reveal a wondrous and complex world.

GROUND FLOOR

CONSTITUTION AVENUE

A grand, two-story space, the Constitution Avenue lobby features three soaring Haida and Tsimshian crest columns opposite a carved stone disk, or *rai*, from the Micronesian island of Yap. Just beyond the entryway, a *Tyrannosaurus rex* skull and a carved ancestor figure from Easter Island flank the pathway leading to the visitor information desk, gift shops, and the

OPPOSITE: Seemingly endless drawers of insects surround museum entomologists. More than 35 million insect specimens are in the museum's collection.

BELOW: An Easter Island *moai* stands sentry near the museum entrance.

Atrium Café. Baird Auditorium, used for lectures, concerts, films, and other special events, is also located on the ground floor. Just outside the auditorium, the *Birds of the District of Columbia* exhibit displays nearly 500 mounted species of birds recorded in the area around Washington, DC.

Q?RIUS

Q?rius (pronounced "curious"), *The Coralyn W. Whitney Science Education Center* is a new way for visitors of all ages to connect science with everyday experiences. The 10,000-square-foot interactive, experimental learning space brings the museum's unique assets—the science, researchers, and collections—out from behind the scenes. Through conversations with scientists and hands-on interactions with thousands of authentic specimens and objects, visitors will enhance their grasp of the natural world, awaken new interests, and build skills for inquiry. Q?rius is part laboratory, part collections vault, part do-it-yourself workshop, and part town square— where visitors can experience natural history in a whole new way: as alive, fun, relevant, and theirs.

FIRST FLOOR

ROTUNDA

Dominating the Rotunda is the largest mounted elephant in the world. This African bull elephant stands 13 feet 2 inches high at the shoulder and weighed close to 12 tons when alive. Surrounding the elephant, visitors can look into a miniature diorama of the elephant in its natural habitat, feel the low rumbles normally unheard by humans that elephants make to communicate over many miles, see how elephants are related to their distant, now-extinct ancestors, and learn about elephant conservation efforts. The visitor information desk is located just under the shadow of the elephant.

On the second-floor balcony encircling the Rotunda, interpretive exhibits look more closely at the elephant's anatomy, evolution, and role in African cultures. The eight-sided Rotunda is one of Washington, DC's most dramatic spaces, and many of its distinctive design elements are best seen from the balcony.

LEFT: Students examine real specimens and investigate scientific questions in Q?rius.

OPPOSITE: The museum's African bull elephant welcomes visitors to the majestic four-story Rotunda.

OCEAN HALL

From the moment visitors arrive in the *Sant Ocean Hall*, they find themselves in another world. A gigantic whale dives overhead, and a vast array of fossils, specimens, and habitats invites exploration. Earth, the exhibit shows, is an ocean planet, with much of its surface covered by a magnificent swath of blue. Though the ocean spans many basins, Earth has only one ocean, and it forms a global system essential to all life on the planet—including yours!

Opened in 2008, the exhibition fills one of the museum's three magnificently restored 24,000-square-foot grand halls. Ongoing research and the museum's unparalleled collections anchor the exhibits; a mix of videos, interactive displays, and new technology for exploring the ocean draws visitors of all ages.

Phoenix, a model of an actual North Atlantic right whale tracked since birth, greets visitors. Descending through the soaring, three-story atrium, she is accurate in every detail. Only about 400 whales like her are left in the world. Below the giant model, a display of hunting and ceremonial artifacts from indigenous Arctic communities reflects their respect for the whale and her gifts of food, fuel, and bone. Three magnificent fossil whales nearby chart the whale's evolution and help transition visitors into the Journey Through Time Gallery, which takes visitors back to 3.7 billion years ago when the first life forms appeared in the sea. Over time, marine species rose and fell in bursts of adaptation and extinction as ocean

ecosystems changed, a process captured by the dramatic murals and fossils.

Two shows play at opposite ends of the hall—one in the Ocean Explorer Theater, where visitors watch a manned submersible dive to the largely unknown sea floor, and the other on a six-foot-wide globe suspended in the Science on a Sphere Gallery. A dramatic multimedia presentation uses data from satellite observations to illuminate the surface of the sphere, showing how the ocean functions as one huge global system.

The hall also invites visitors to become ocean explorers. In the open ocean, they find marine organisms living in three layers: sunlit surface, twilight zone (where food and light are scarce), and cold, dark ocean bottom. On the coastline—where humans have the most impact on the ocean—a look beneath a beach blanket reveals an amazing variety of microscopic animals wedged between grains of sand. The 1,500-gallon aquarium holds a live Indo-Pacific reef with dozens of colorful species.

BELOW LEFT: The living coral reef in the *Sant Ocean Hall* supports a rich diversity of marine life, from fishes to crustaceans.

BELOW RIGHT: Visitors can discover the ocean in all its complexity and unearthly beauty in the *Sant Ocean Hall*.

HUMAN ORIGINS HALL

Who are we? Who were our ancestors? When did they live?

The museum's groundbreaking *David H. Koch Hall of Human Origins*, which opened in 2010, explores these universal questions and reveals how the characteristics that make us human evolved against a backdrop of dramatic climate change. The story begins over 6 million years ago on the African continent, where the earliest humans took the first steps toward walking upright. Since then, more than a dozen species of early humans have existed, with multiple species often sharing the planet. All of them are now extinct—except for our own, *Homo sapiens.*

The exhibition tells this incredible story through more than 280 fossils, casts, and artifacts, many from the museum's own collections. Displayed alongside the research of the Smithsonian Human Origins program and other scientific institutions, the objects trace the evolutionary history of our small branch of the tree of life.

Visitors enter the hall through a time tunnel, seeing nine early human species appear and disappear and environments come and go. Along one large wall, a dramatic display of fossils, objects, videos, and images features some of the most significant "milestones" in our path to becoming human: walking upright, making tools, evolving different body types and larger brains, developing social networks, and creating symbols and language.

Three displays re-create specific moments in the past and invite visitors to explore actual excavations. The braincase of a 1.8-million-year-old youth found in Swartkrans, South Africa, for example, still shows a leopard's fatal

puncture marks. Visitors reconstruct the scene as they touch models of fossil "clues" from the site, and the life-and-death events of that fateful day long ago unfold in a time-lapse animation.

At the crossroads of the hall, a fascinating display of fossil skulls illustrates the history of human evolution. Nearby, eight lifelike faces stare out at visitors. Artist John Gurche worked for more than two years to sculpt the faces, using the latest forensic techniques, fossil discoveries, and his knowledge of human and ape anatomy. Gurche also created the hall's five life-sized bronze sculptures of different early human species doing activities such as making a fire or gathering food.

Our species, *Homo sapiens,* evolved in East Africa by around 300,000 years ago, and then—as a world map of fossil discoveries shows—spread around the globe. Physical and cultural differences emerged as populations adapted to different habitats. Still, despite superficial variations in size, shape, skin, and eyes, the DNA among all modern humans differs by only 0.1 percent.

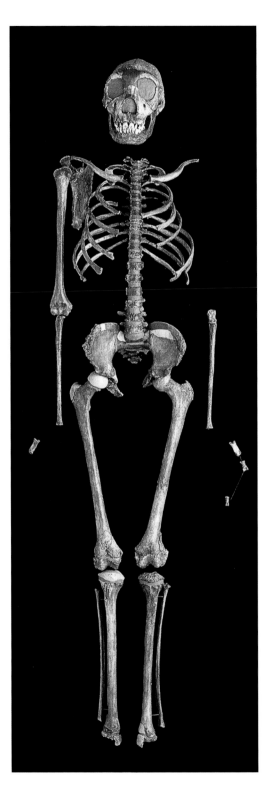

LEFT: The skeleton of Turkana Boy, a juvenile *Homo erectus*, was found in 1.6-million-year-old sediments west of Lake Turkana, Kenya.

OPPOSITE TOP: This reconstruction of "Lucy," a 3.2-million-year-old female *Australopithecus afarensis*, was sculpted by John Gurche.

OPPOSITE BELOW: The exhibit displays many reproductions of Paleolithic paintings and sculptures, including the 17,000-year-old yellow "Chinese Horse" from Lascaux Cave, France.

MAMMALS HALL

The *Kenneth E. Behring Family Hall of Mammals* invites you to join the mammal family reunion. Dramatic displays set against the hall's impressive original architecture present the wondrous diversity of mammals and tell the story of how they adapted to a changing world. As the exhibition demonstrates, all mammals past and present—visitors included—are related to one another by virtue of common descent. Mammals belong to an ancient lineage that stretches back to the time before dinosaurs. Living mammals all share certain characteristics that scientists use to identify the group. Mammals have hair, nurse on milk, and have a unique hearing apparatus that evolved from ancestral jawbones. We are all part of the great diversity of mammals.

The hall combines a passionate and detailed commitment to scholarship with fresh interpretive approaches to engage and educate visitors. The exhibition features the museum's collections and takes full advantage of new interactive learning technologies, which offer in-depth perspectives on scientific content. Designed with families in mind, the exhibit showcases taxidermy mammals in exciting, lifelike poses and features a wealth of hands-on activities. An award-winning theater presentation documents mammal evolution.

Visit the grasslands, deserts, and forests of Africa: get up close to a giraffe, see how lions hunt large prey, and learn about bears that lived here more than 5 million years ago. Wander through Australia, where ancient mammals flourished and today is the only place in the world inhabited by all

three mammal groups: monotremes, marsupials, and placentals. Visit North America's far north and see how mammals protect themselves from the cold. Then travel to North American woodlands and prairies and observe how beavers make their homes and how the pronghorn runs faster than any other living mammal. Discover the world of the Amazon rain forest, the Earth's largest, where abundant plant life sets the stage for crowded living conditions. Find out how rain forest mammals make the most of these resources, from the shady forest floor to the canopy above.

If you really want to get to know your relatives, the *Kenneth E. Behring Hall of Mammals* is the place to go!

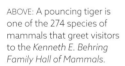

ABOVE: A pouncing tiger is one of the 274 species of mammals that greet visitors to the *Kenneth E. Behring Family Hall of Mammals.*

RIGHT: North America's largest living carnivore, the brown bear looks similar to its 250,000-year-old ancestors.

FOSSIL HALL

Following the largest renovation ever undertaken at the museum, the *David H. Koch Hall of Fossils—Deep Time* exhibition opened in 2019. Inside, more than 700 specimens tell the dramatic story of life's 3.7-billion-year history. Arranged by time period, the gallery's displays highlight the connections between ecosystems, climate, geological forces, and evolution and encourage visitors to understand that the choices they make today will have an impact on the future.

Visitors entering the exhibition from the Rotunda are invited to journey from the age of mammals back to the origins of life on Earth. Entering from the other end of the exhibition, just beyond *African Voices*, visitors start with early life and work their way to the present. Throughout the hall, you can peek into miniature dioramas and glimpse snapshots of past ecosystems. "Human Connections" stories link the deep past to today, and the raised platform overlooking the main gallery carries a clear message: we are causing rapid, unprecedented change to the climate, ecosystems, and life on our planet. But as the videos and interactives in this area show, there is hope—we can adapt, innovate, and collaborate to leave a positive legacy.

Starting with the most recent ice ages, visitors can learn how climate fluctuations and human expansion changed the world. Next, travel back to the Neogene and Paleogene periods, where mammals diversified in new landscapes left open by the extinction of dinosaurs, from towering rain forests to vast grasslands. Three central platforms showcase the Cretaceous, Jurassic, and Triassic periods—the age of dinosaurs, bookended by two of the most dramatic mass extinction events in Earth's history. You can explore the Permian displays to discover how today's familiar food webs formed, or step into a coal mine to learn how Carboniferous swamps fossilized and turned into coal. As you round the corner, time speeds up, covering more than 90 percent of Earth's 4.6-billion-year history, from the first life forms that arose in the ocean 3.7 billion years ago to the first plants and animals to move ashore.

In addition to the many videos, interactives, and tactile displays throughout the hall, visitors can get more hands-on experiences in Fossil Basecamp, an interactive space that explores how Earth works, how life evolves, how fossils form, and how scientists find and date fossils. The nearby FossiLab shows how scientists and volunteers prepare fossils for our collections and displays.

LEFT: Visitors can look behind the scenes as museum staff and volunteers prepare fossils in the FossiLab, an active workspace.

OPPOSITE: The Nation's *T. rex* reigns over the museum's new fossil hall—and over the *Triceratops* carcass. *Credit:* Courtesy of the US Army Corps of Engineers, Omaha District and The Museum of the Rockies, Montana State University.

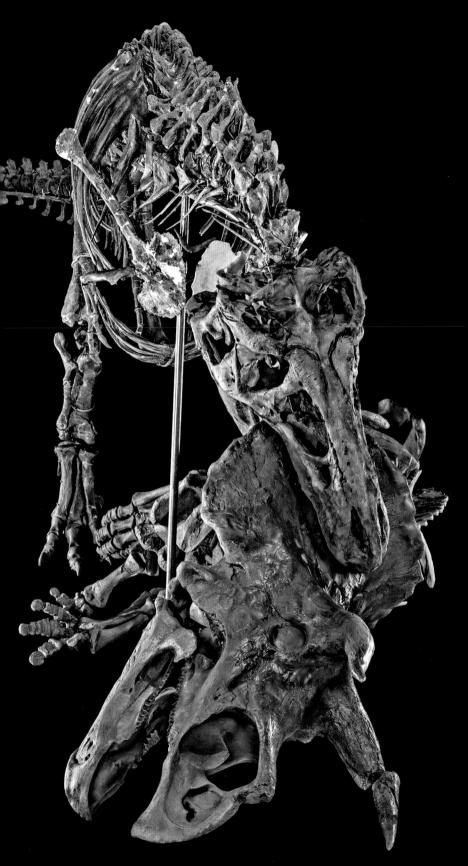

AFRICAN VOICES

Rich and resonant voices from Africa and the African diaspora—together with objects both commonplace and extraordinary—express the complexity of African lives and cultures. Africa's most striking characteristics are its immense size and diverse cultures. More than three times larger than the continental United States, Africa today is home to more than a billion people inhabiting 54 countries. The African continent is divided by the boundaries of its nation-states as well as by diverse language groups, cultures, ecological zones, and histories.

The *African Voices* exhibition resonates with the dynamism of contemporary African cultures. It examines the overlapping, continuously broadening spheres of African influence—historical and contemporary, local and international—in the realms of family, work, commerce, and the natural environment. Objects such as a 17th-century cast-brass head from the Benin Kingdom of Nigeria, a late-19th-century carved wooden staff by the Luba of Zaire, and decorative fiber headwear from 19th- and 20th-century Zaire show the aesthetic dimensions of leadership in certain African societies.

A late-19th-century copper-and-brass image made by the Kota peoples of Gabon and a contemporary Afro-Brazilian altar demonstrate the enduring presence of African belief systems on the African continent and in Africa's diaspora. Akan gold weights, Ethiopian silver crosses, and decorated ceramic vessels show the history of metallurgy and pottery in different regions.

Objects used in everyday life, contemporary fashion, children's toys, musical instruments, and excerpts from oral poetry, song, and literary texts illustrate the transatlantic connection between Africa and the Americas.

RIGHT: This 18th-century brass head of an *oba*, or king, comes from the Benin Kingdom, now a part of Nigeria. The opening on top once held a carved ivory tusk depicting the glories of the *oba*'s reign.

OPPOSITE TOP: The 45.52-carat Hope Diamond is the best-known and largest blue diamond in the world.

OPPOSITE BOTTOM: This rare Moon rock is one of a series of displays showing the different stages of the Moon's formation.

SECOND FLOOR
GEOLOGY, GEMS, AND MINERALS HALL

The *Janet Annenberg Hooker Hall of Geology, Gems, and Minerals*, located off the second-floor Rotunda balcony, is among the world's most comprehensive overviews of earth science. The legendary Hope Diamond—a must-see for visitors—stars in the Harry Winston Gallery. Surrounded by sparkling white diamonds, the 45.52-carat blue diamond rotates in a custom-made vault under precise fiber-optic lighting. The gem is named for former owner Henry Philip Hope of England and is still in the setting made for Evelyn Walsh McLean of Washington, DC, its last private owner. Harry Winston, Inc., the New York jewelry firm, acquired the famous diamond in 1949 and donated it to the Smithsonian in 1958.

The Harry Winston Gallery also features five other wonders of nature: enormous quartz crystals from Africa, one of the largest sheets of naturally occurring copper in existence, a sandstone formation sculpted by water within the Earth, polished gneiss born from heat and pressure deep below the surface, and a ring-shaped meteorite from another world. The National Gem Collection includes the Marie Antoinette diamond earrings, the 127-carat octagonal Asscher Portuguese diamond, and the 75.47-carat Hooker emerald. The 2,500 specimens in the Gems and Minerals Gallery include spectacular crystal pockets, a dazzling selection of gems, and crystals that have grown in amazing and unusual ways.

In the Rocks Gallery, each specimen represents a bit of Earth's history and shows how rocks bend, break, melt, and transform into other kinds of rocks over time. Intense heat from within the Earth drives the movement of rocky plates at the surface—the process highlighted in the Plate Tectonics Gallery with specimens from volcanoes and earthquakes, a volcano study station, and a theater. Completing the hall, the Moon, Meteorites, and Solar System Gallery features Moon rocks, a touchable Mars meteorite, an extensive display of other meteorites, and tiny bits of stardust from the cloud that gave birth to the Sun.

ABOVE: Young visitors encounter butterflies up close in the Butterfly Pavilion.

BELOW: A rose swallowtail butterfly folds its brightly colored wings as it hangs out on a leaf.

OPPOSITE: At the popular Insect Zoo, you can get close enough to see the hairs on a tarantula. Tarantulas use their hairs to locate prey.

BUTTERFLY PAVILION

No matter what season you visit, it feels like a picture-perfect summer day inside the *Partners in Evolution: Butterflies + Plants* exhibition. Hundreds of butterflies and moths flutter from flower to flower, sip nectar, roost, and flex their wings. Small chrysalides hang in the Emergence Chamber just as they would in nature, while caterpillars' tissues reorganize and adult butterflies take shape. The butterflies and moths come in a stunning variety of colors and patterns, which helps protect them from predators. Look for moths that match the bark where they roost, conspicuous wing patterns that advertise a bitter taste, and eye spots on wings that help frighten away birds and lizards. Tickets for the Pavilion are available online at naturalhistory.si.edu/exhibits/butterfly-pavilion or at the Pavilion box office.

There is no charge to see the many other displays in the exhibition, where visitors discover more about how butterflies and moths live and how they evolved with plants over hundreds of millions of years. Sometimes butterflies and plants interact as friends, sometimes as foes. Take the yucca moth and yucca plant: for some 40 million years, yucca moths have played an important role in fertilizing yucca plants while depositing their eggs in the yucca flowers' ovaries.

A series of murals and rare plant and insect fossils paint images of Earth in four different time periods, showing how tens of millions of years of evolution produced the amazing diversity of butterflies and moths seen today. Along the way, many species died out, while others endured, eventually giving rise to the specialized day-flying moths we now call butterflies.

A display near the Rotunda entrance gives a sense of just how large the museum's plant, insect, and fossil collections are and shows the critical role they play as museum scientists work to unravel the mysteries of evolution.

INSECT ZOO

The whirs, chirps, buzzes, and rattles heard at the entrance to the *O. Orkin Insect Zoo* are the sounds of Earth's most abundant, diverse, and successful animals—insects and their relatives. They have adapted extraordinarily well to environments all over the world, from deserts and mangrove swamps to tropical rainforests—and even inside our homes.

The interactive exhibits and participatory activities in the Insect Zoo invite visitors of all ages to explore and get involved. Children can crawl through a large model of an African termite mound, watch butterflies hatch, or hold a hissing cockroach. Tarantula feedings take place several times a day.

BONES HALL

The hundreds of skeletons in this hall introduce you to the vertebrates—fishes, amphibians, reptiles, birds, and mammals (including you). These animals all have an internal skeleton with a backbone, but as different kinds of vertebrates adapted to new habitats, seemingly endless variations on the basic skeletal structure evolved. Characteristic poses and cutaway views show the function and composition of different bone structures. You can compare the similarities and differences between groups—for example, the wings of bats, a type of mammal, versus those of birds, the descendants of dinosaurs.

ANCIENT EGYPT

In the *Eternal Life in Ancient Egypt* exhibition, mummies, their burial wraps, and their tomb objects provide dramatic evidence of life (and death) in an ancient culture that lasted for more than 3,000 years. Mummies are the remains of real people who hoped to live forever by keeping their bodies intact and equipping their tombs with everything they might need in the next life, from cosmetics to plates for food. One of the mummies on display lies in its original coffin, with a golden mask and painted fragments of papier-mâché ornamenting the head and body.

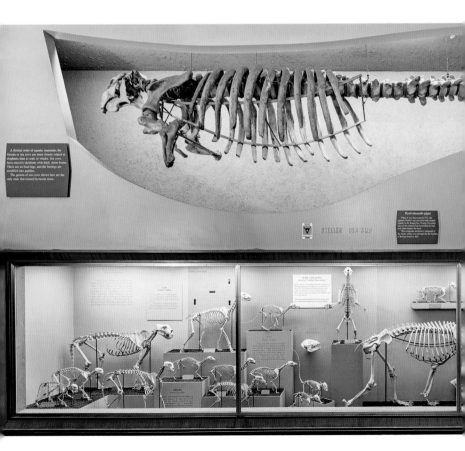

BELOW: The massive skeleton of a Steller's sea cow looms over skeletons of meat-eating mammals. It was assembled from bones salvaged on Bering Island in 1883—except for its missing front flippers.

RIGHT: This coffin belonged to Tentkhonsu, a woman from an elite family who sang at the temple in Thebes and served the god Khonsu.

EXTRAS

The Nation's *T. rex*, the Hope Diamond, the African bull elephant, and the huge North Atlantic right whale are among the most popular exhibits in this museum, but don't miss out on these other experiences.

GARDEN LOUNGE

On the museum's second floor, visitors can rest and recharge themselves and their phones among live plants. This airy, light-filled space, tucked away from the hustle and bustle of the rest of the museum, features benches and charging stations with outlets, as well as lush displays of living flowers, ferns, and cycads. Explore how plants "move," or disperse, to survive and thrive. Discover how plants are vital to all land ecosystems, and to human lives. Look for *Vanilla planifolia*, the orchid that gives us vanilla "beans." Or just breathe in deeply, sit, and relax.

RIGHT: This life-size model of a mega-toothed shark was installed in the museum's newly renovated dining spaces in 2019.

BELOW: Visitors sit and chat—or rest—amid the greenery in *The Garden Lounge*.

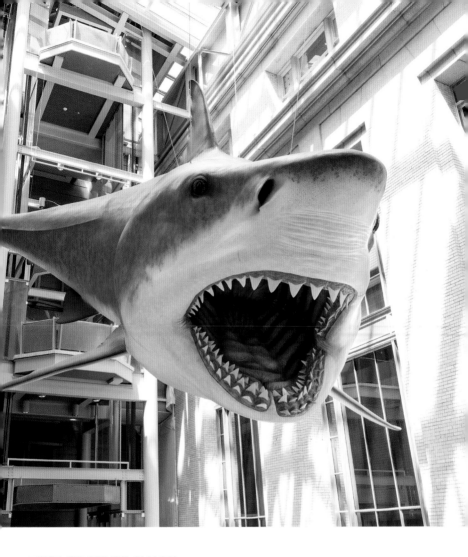

MEGA-TOOTHED SHARK

Step out onto the walkway connecting the Ocean Hall with the Ocean Terrace Café and come face-to-face with a 52-foot-long model shark suspended in the atrium. And not just any shark—it's *Carcharocles megalodon*, the largest predatory shark of all time. This extinct fish is often called simply "megalodon" for its giant teeth, which it used to devour small baleen whales, seals, sea turtles, and large fishes. You can touch a bronze cast of one of its serrated teeth before grabbing your own bite to eat at the café.

Before it went extinct 3.6 million years ago, *Carcharocles* prowled warm, shallow seas around the globe, including the Chesapeake Bay region—it may even have swum through the waters where the museum is today.

SPECIAL EXHIBITIONS

There's always something new to see at the museum. From world-class photography displays to new discoveries and environmental issues in a rapidly changing world, the National Museum of Natural History offers an exciting roster of changing exhibitions every year. The exhibitions amplify the museum's mission of explaining the natural world and our place in it, and they complement its research and educational goals.

The museum hosts traveling exhibitions from other institutions as well as those developed by our own exhibits and curatorial staff. Many exhibitions reflect the cutting-edge science and research conducted at the museum.

ABOVE: *Outbreak!* brings together epidemiologists, veterinarians, public health workers, and citizens across the globe as they work to identify and contain infectious diseases.

LEFT and OPPOSITE: Discover the story behind these shoebills, this samurai armor, and hundreds of other items from our collections in *Objects of Wonder*.

GENERAL INFORMATION

INFORMATION SERVICES

The visitor information desks, located near the Constitution Avenue entrance and in the Rotunda, are staffed by volunteers daily from 10 a.m. to 4 p.m. Call 202-633-1000 (voice) or 202-357-1729 (non-voice TTY) or go online to naturalhistory.si.edu.

ACCESSIBILITY

The museum is wheelchair accessible at both the Constitution Avenue and Madison Drive entrances. Accessibility information is available at naturalhistory.si.edu/visit/accessibility, and by calling (202) 633-5238 or emailing NMNHAccessibility@si.edu. Wheelchairs are available for free on a first-come, first-served basis. Many exhibitions include tactile experiences, and exhibit videos are captioned. Loop amplification is available on Highlights Tours, at both information desks, and for the Worldwide Theater in the Human Origins Hall. Assisted listening devices are available on Highlights Tours and in the Age of Humans theater in the Fossil Hall. The Fossil Hall has a companion app called Deep Time Audio Description, available for free download on visitors' personal mobile devices. Sign-language interpretation, real-time captioning, and tactile tours are available with advance notice. For special services for groups, call 202-633-5238 or email NMNHAccessibility@si.edu.

TOURS

The National Museum of Natural History offers visitors free guided tours and hands-on Q?rius stations located throughout the museum, both presented by our dynamic and knowledgeable volunteers. Walk-in Highlights Tours of the exhibitions and collections are given Mondays through Fridays at 10:30 a.m. and 1:30 p.m. (except on some holidays). Meet in the Rotunda, Mall entrance. Tours are subject to volunteer availability; last-minute cancellations may occur, so please check with the visitor information desks.

14-01 Fishes and Amphibians

15-01 Birds

14-02 Reptiles

Turtles

15-02 Birds

DINING
The 500-seat Atrium Café, located on the ground floor, features craft burgers, flatbreads, pastas, and a Chef's Market table. The Ocean Terrace Café on the first floor seats 200 and offers seasonal vegetable-focused entrees and sandwiches, specialty coffees, dessert, and locally crafted gelato. Both dining areas provide views of the life-size model of the mega-toothed shark.

SHOPPING
The Gallery Store on the ground floor carries a variety of Smithsonian souvenirs and gifts related to natural history, as well as a bookstore. Across the hall, the Family Store specializes in educational and fun items for children and adults. Theme-oriented shops elsewhere in the museum include the Gem and Mineral Store (second floor) and the Dinos and More Store (first floor).

LIVE BUTTERFLY PAVILION
Open daily 10:15 a.m. to 5 p.m. Tickets are required and are available online at naturalhistory.si.edu/exhibits/butterfly-pavilion and at the second-floor Pavilion box office. Tuesdays are free, but a timed-entry ticket is required and available only at the Pavilion box office.

LIVE DEMONSTRATIONS
Tarantula feedings in the *O. Orkin Insect Zoo*, Monday through Friday, 10:30 a.m., 11:30 a.m., and 1:30 p.m.; Saturday and Sunday, 11:30 a.m., 12:30 p.m., and 1:30 p.m.

Q?RIUS, THE CORALYN W. WHITNEY SCIENCE EDUCATION CENTER
Q?rius is an evolving learning lab on the ground floor of the museum. This interactive learning space for visitors of all ages brings science to life. Visitors can use microscopes, handle collection objects, solve science puzzles, and even meet a scientist. During the summer, it is open to the public daily from 10 a.m. until 5 p.m. From October through June, school programs are available Monday through Friday with reservations during morning hours. Please consult the website for hours and programming.

ABOVE: The museum's entrance on Constitution Avenue is within walking distance of two Metro stations and several bus lines.

OPPOSITE: The collections in Q?rius inspire new ways of looking at the natural world.

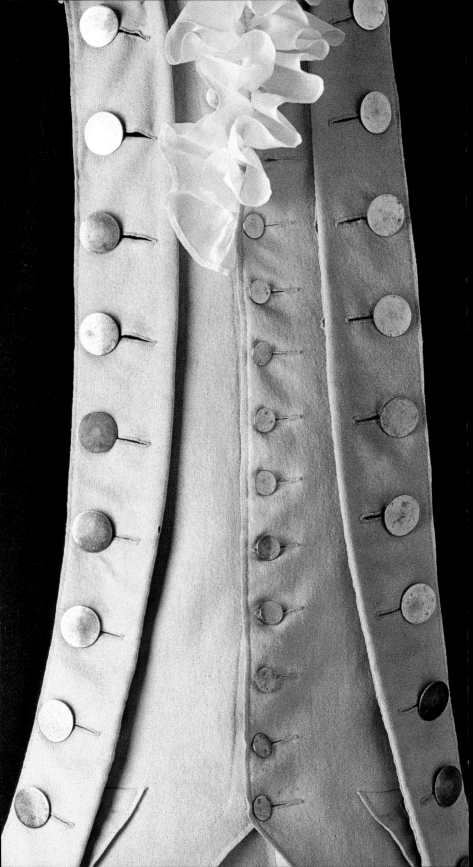

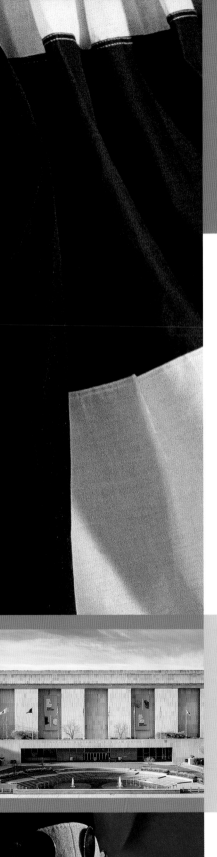

NATIONAL MUSEUM OF AMERICAN HISTORY
BEHRING CENTER

The Star-Spangled Banner, the First Ladies' gowns, Abraham Lincoln's hat, Lewis and Clark's compass, Muhammad Ali's boxing gloves, Thomas Jefferson's portable writing desk on which he wrote the Declaration of Independence, the John Bull locomotive, Dorothy's Ruby Slippers from the *Wizard of Oz*—the list of America's favorites goes on and on in the museum's wide-ranging, entertaining, and educational collections.

OPPOSITE: General George Washington began wearing this uniform coat around 1789, after he had resigned from the Continental army to become the nation's commander in chief.

Constitution Avenue between 12th and 14th Streets NW

Mall entrance: Madison Drive between 12th and 14th Streets NW

Open daily from 10 a.m. to 5:30 p.m. Closed December 25

Metrorail: Federal Triangle or Smithsonian station

Smithsonian information: 202-633-1000 americanhistory.si.edu

In 1858, the "objects of art and of foreign and curious research" in the national cabinet of curiosities were transferred from the US Patent Office to the Smithsonian Institution. This was the genesis of the collections in the National Museum of American History. After the Centennial Exposition of 1876 closed, the Smithsonian received a windfall of objects that had been displayed in Philadelphia for the nation's 100th anniversary celebration.

Many of those objects were put on exhibit in the US National Museum Building (now the Arts and Industries Building) when it opened in 1881. Today the spacious halls of the National Museum of American History are filled with exhibits that explore America's social, cultural, scientific, and technological history—with the goal of becoming the most accessible, inclusive, relevant, and sustainable history museum in the nation.

Visitors immediately connect to the American story as they walk into the museum's central atrium from the Mall. In 2008, as part of a major renovation, the museum transformed how its audiences experience history—through new exhibitions, learning places, and programming spaces. A skylight dramatically opens the building, and a grand staircase connects the museum's first and second floors. The Nina and Ivan Selin Welcome Center, adjacent to the Mall entrance, helps visitors make the most of their time at the museum by providing easy access to information about exhibitions, tours, programs, and amenities.

For more information, visit the museum's website, americanhistory.si.edu.

FIRST FLOOR
TRANSPORTATION AND TECHNOLOGY

AMERICA ON THE MOVE

This 26,000-square-foot exhibition anchors the General Motors Hall of Transportation and features more than 300 transportation artifacts—from the 1903 Winton, the first car to be driven across the USA, to the 199-ton, 92-foot-long "1401" locomotive, to a 1970s shipping container—all showcased in period settings.

SMITHSONIAN LIBRARIES GALLERY

The Smithsonian Libraries Exhibition Gallery is located on the first floor in the west wing of the National Museum of American History. Curated by Smithsonian staff, the exhibition space showcases items from the libraries' rich and diverse collections. For more information, see page 32.

LEFT: The *Fredonia's* deep hull, narrow beam, and fine lines represent the pinnacle of design for deepwater fishing schooners. In 1896, the *Fredonia* was hit by a heavy sea and sank.

BELOW: The John Bull is the world's oldest operable self-propelled locomotive. The Bull set the style for American locomotives to come.

The exhibition's nineteen settings, organized chronologically, allow visitors the opportunity to travel back in time and experience transportation as it shaped American lives and landscapes. As visitors travel through the show, they can walk on 40 feet of Route 66's original pavement from Oklahoma or board a 1950s Chicago Transit Authority Car and, through multimedia technology, experience a "commute" into downtown Chicago.

ON THE WATER

An 8,000-square-foot exhibition about the country's maritime history and culture, *On the Water: Stories from Maritime America* engages the public in a dynamic exploration of America's maritime past and present through objects, video, and interactive stations.

LANDMARK OBJECT: JOHN BULL LOCOMOTIVE

The oldest operable self-propelled locomotive in the world, the John Bull became a symbol of the Industrial Revolution. Built in England and brought to America in 1831 for service on the Camden and Amboy Railroad of New Jersey, one of the first public railroads in the United States, the John Bull was an English design modified to fit the expansion of a frontier nation. The locomotive transported passengers between two of America's largest cities, Philadelphia and New York.

WARNER BROS. THEATER

The Warner Bros. Theater, near the Constitution Avenue entrance, is a state-of-the-art venue for public programs, including film screenings, lectures, concerts, and symposia. Check the information desk or visit the museum's website for the current schedule.

LIGHTING A REVOLUTION

Thomas Edison's revolutionary invention is only the beginning of the story of electricity, the subject of this exhibition. Here visitors can explore the similarities and differences between the processes of invention in Edison's era and today.

POWER MACHINERY

The full-size engines and models displayed here illustrate the harnessing of atmospheric forces, the early age of steam power, and the development of high-pressure and high-speed engines. Displays show the evolution of steam boilers and the steam turbine, and progress in the techniques of harnessing waterpower. The collection also includes historic internal-combustion engines.

BIG MONEY

This display presents visitors with "big" money; that is, money in large quantities, sizes, and denominations. Featured objects from the National Numismatic Collection include a portion of the Confederate currency hoard, Swedish plate money, and German billion-mark bank notes that focus on economic and monetary ideas.

LEFT: Thomas Edison used this carbon-filament bulb in the first public demonstration of his most famous invention—the light bulb, the first practical electric incandescent lamp.

OPPOSITE: Julia Child's kitchen from her home in Cambridge, Massachusetts, where three of her TV series were filmed, is on display at the museum.

¡PRESENTE! A LATINO HISTORY OF THE UNITED STATES

The Smithsonian Latino Center will open its first gallery space, the Molina Family Latino Gallery, in 2022 at the National Museum of American History. *¡Presente! A Latino History of the United States*, the inaugural exhibition, tells American history from the perspectives of the diverse Latinos who lived it. This exhibition uncovers hidden and forgotten stories, connects visitors to Latino culture, and lays the foundation for understanding how Latinos inform and shape US history.

FOOD: TRANSFORMING THE AMERICAN TABLE

This exhibition examines some of the major changes in food and wine in postwar America. From the impact of new technologies to the influence of social and cultural shifts, the exhibition considers how these factors helped transform food and its production, preparation, and consumption as well as what we know about what's good for us. The public is invited to take a seat at a large communal table in the center of the exhibition to share thoughts and experiences about food and change in America.

JULIA CHILD'S KITCHEN

Julia Child's home kitchen, with its hundreds of tools, appliances, and furnishings, serves as the opening story in the museum's first major exhibition on food history.

INVENTION AND INNOVATION

On the west side of the building, explore the museum's Innovation Wing, which has more than a dozen exhibitions, hands-on learning spaces, and places for programs.

INVENTING IN AMERICA: JOHN LOUIS GATEWAY TO INNOVATION

The introduction to the theme of innovation begins in the concourse area leading to the west wing. Here, in collaboration with the US Patent and Trademark Office, *Inventing in America* focuses on inventions and innovators of the past and present, including Alexander Graham Bell, Thomas Edison, and Samuel Morse. The display features early patent models as well as trademarks and inventions of National Inventors Hall of Fame members.

LANDMARK OBJECT: RALPH BAER'S INVENTOR'S WORKSHOP

Ralph H. Baer, known as the inventor of the home video game, donated his workshop to the museum. This exhibit introduces visitors to the theme of innovation through gaming technology.

OPPOSITE: The Teddy bear was created by the Ideal Toy Company and named after Theodore Roosevelt in 1903.

BELOW: The first floor of the west wing focuses on innovation and creativity. The Manchester, New Hampshire, workshop of Ralph H. Baer, a prolific inventor who was often referred to as the "father of video games," is the landmark object here.

MARS HALL OF AMERICAN BUSINESS: AMERICAN ENTERPRISE

American Enterprise chronicles the tumultuous interaction of capitalism and democracy that resulted in the continual remaking of American business—and American life. Visitors are immersed in the dramatic arc of power, wealth, success, and failure in America in an 8,000-square-foot space centered on the role of business and innovation from the mid-1700s to the present and tracing the country's development from a small, dependent, agricultural nation to one of the world's most vibrant economies. In addition to a chronological and thematic approach, the exhibition focuses on advertising history and features a biography

wall with inventors, entrepreneurs, marketers, regulators, and others who have influenced and changed the marketplace. The show concludes with "The Exchange," a section of the exhibition with interactive and hands-on opportunities for visitors.

SPARK!LAB

Spark!Lab is where museum visitors become inventors. The Lemelson Center for the Study of Invention and Innovation invites children ages 6–12 to create, collaborate, explore, test, experiment, and invent. Activities for children and families incorporate traditional science, technology, engineering, and math (STEM) with art, museum activities, and creativity.

THE JEROME AND DOROTHY LEMELSON HALL OF INVENTION AND INNOVATION: PLACES OF INVENTION

Places of Invention takes visitors on a journey through time and place across America to discover the stories of six inspiring communities. A focus on precision manufacturing in Hartford, Connecticut, in the late 1800s shows how a factory town puts the pieces together in explosive new ways. The story of Technicolor in Hollywood, California, in the 1930s puts the spotlight on the young town that gave birth to the golden age of movies.

An examination of cardiac innovations of the 1950s in Medical Alley, Minnesota, reveals how a tight-knit community of tinkerers keeps hearts ticking. A look at hip-hop's birth in the Bronx, New York, in the 1970s shows how neighborhood ingenuity created new beats. The rise of the personal computer in Silicon Valley, California, in the 1970s–1980s reminds us of how suburban garage hackers plus lab researchers led to personal computing. Through clean-energy innovations in Fort Collins, Colorado, a college town combines its energies for a greener planet.

INVENTIVE MINDS

Inventive Minds, adjacent to *Places of Invention*, introduces visitors to the mission and work of the Lemelson Center, particularly its efforts to document invention. Brief video interviews of inventors, complemented by archival materials and artifacts, puts the focus on the people, who tell their stories in their own words—and their processes. The gallery also highlights the inventive creativity of Jerome Lemelson and the vision of Lemelson and his wife, Dorothy, in founding the Lemelson Center at the Smithsonian in 1995.

PATRICK F. TAYLOR FOUNDATION: OBJECT PROJECT

Object Project presents familiar objects in a new light, exploring how people, innovations, and social change shaped life as we know it. Visitors have the opportunity to see and handle objects—from refrigerators and bicycles to ready-to-wear clothing and household conveniences as diverse as window screens and deodorant—and explore their significance through historic documents and compelling activities. Encompassing almost 4,000 square feet, the display features some 300 objects, including a "magic" scrapbook and a special version of *The Price Is Right*, and offers visitors the chance to try on clothing virtually.

WEGMANS WONDERPLACE

This space allows curious kids ages five and under to "cook" in a kitchen inspired by Julia Child; plant and harvest pretend vegetables and run the farm stand; find the owls hiding in a miniature replica of the Smithsonian's Castle building; and captain a tugboat based on a model in the museum's collection. Here we nurture the motivation behind innovation—the sense of wonder that causes us to ask why, or why not.

DOLLHOUSE

Faith Bradford donated this dollhouse to the Smithsonian in 1951 after spending more than a half century collecting and building its miniature furnishings. The dollhouse family includes Peter Doll, his wife, Rose Washington Doll, and their 10 children.

GALLERY OF NUMISMATICS:
THE VALUE OF MONEY

A vault door marks the entrance to *The Value of Money*, where visitors delve into the National Numismatic Collection to explore the origins of money, new monetary technologies, the political and cultural messages money conveys, numismatic art and design, and the practice of collecting money. It features more than 400 objects from the collection, including a storied 1933 Double Eagle, an 1849 $20 gold coin, a 1934 $100,000 note, and a Depression-era one-dollar clamshell.

OPPOSITE: *Object Project* is an exhibition about everyday things that changed everything.

ABOVE: Live cooking demonstrations occur monthly on the Wallace H. Coulter Performance Plaza in the Innovation Wing. Check the museum's website to learn more about Cooking Up History and see the current schedule.

WALLACE H. COULTER
PERFORMANCE PLAZA

Against the backdrop of a dramatic first-floor panoramic window, this performance space and demonstration stage with a working kitchen highlights Americans' quest for the new. Programming is linked to the ideas of innovation presented on the floor as well as to food, music, and theater, through which visitors can better understand American history. Daily schedules are available at americanhistory.si.edu and the information desk.

ARCHIVES CENTER

The museum's Archives Center shows highlights from its collections in changing displays. The center's collections are particularly rich in the areas of technology, consumer culture (including advertising and marketing), invention and innovation, popular music, African American history and culture, and many other topics that document the American experience.

SECOND FLOOR
STAR-SPANGLED BANNER GALLERY

The museum is home to the Star-Spangled Banner, the flag that inspired the national anthem. Visitors are able to view the flag in an atmosphere reminiscent of the "dawn's early light"—what Francis Scott Key experienced on the morning of September 14, 1814—and learn about history and preservation.

LANDMARK OBJECT: GEORGE WASHINGTON STATUE, THE NATION WE BUILD TOGETHER

This marble statue of George Washington was sculpted by Horatio Greenough under commission by the US government in 1832. Designed as an allusion to Phidias's Olympian *Zeus*, the sculpture was originally unveiled in the Capitol Rotunda in 1841 and later moved to the Capitol's lawn. The statue came to the Smithsonian in 1908 and debuted in this building in 1964.

WITHIN THESE WALLS

Within These Walls tells the history of a house that stood at 16 Elm Street in Ipswich, Massachusetts, and five of the many families who occupied it from the mid-1760s through 1945. The exhibition explores some of the important ways that ordinary people, in their daily lives, have been part of the great changes and events in American history. The centerpiece is the largest artifact in the museum: a Georgian-style, two-and-a-half-story, timber-framed house built in the 1760s, saved from the bulldozer by the citizens of Ipswich in 1963, and relocated to this space. Within this house, American colonists created new ways of living, patriots sparked a revolution, an African American struggled for freedom, community activists organized to end slavery, immigrants built new identities for themselves, and a grandmother and her grandson served on the home front during World War II.

MANY VOICES, ONE NATION

This exhibition takes visitors on a chronological and thematic journey that maps the cultural geography of the diverse and complex stories animating the Latin emblem on the country's Great Seal and its national ideal: *E pluribus Unum*—Out of many, one.

OPPOSITE: The marble statue of George Washington, sculpted by Horatio Greenough, welcomes visitors to exhibits on American democracy and culture.

ABOVE: A two-and-a-half-story timber-framed house from 1760 was brought to the museum from Ipswich, Massachusetts, in 1963 and is the centerpiece of the exhibition *Within These Walls.*

AMERICAN DEMOCRACY: THE GREAT LEAP OF FAITH

This exhibition encourages visitors to explore the history of citizen participation, debate, and compromise from the nation's formation through to today. Covering the American past from the Revolution to the present, this exhibition traces the unfolding of this American experiment through the museum's national treasures and representative artifacts to examine our founding political principles, including democracy, freedom, and equality.

NICHOLAS F. AND EUGENIA TAUBMAN GALLERY

This intimate gallery allows the museum to show changing exhibitions on topics that amplify the theme of the floor. Check the museum's website for current information.

ABOVE: Before the ratification of the Twenty-third Amendment in 1961, residents of the District of Columbia could not vote in presidential elections. DC residents used objects like this lapel pin to demand representation at the national level, a request that was only partially granted.

RIGHT: Before Uncle Sam and Lady Liberty were created, Columbia was an idealized feminine figure that personified the new nation of America. Over time, the image of Columbia became a symbol for American ideals during wars such as the American Revolution, the War of 1812, and World War I.

OPPOSITE: Four African American students refused to leave the lunch counter at F. W. Woolworth's in Greensboro, North Carolina, starting a nationwide sit-in movement.

THE WALLACE H. COULTER UNITY SQUARE

Public discourse at the national level takes place in Unity Square, exploring themes related to democracy, immigration, and discovering what it means to be American.

ALBERT H. SMALL DOCUMENTS GALLERY

This intimate gallery allows the museum to show changing displays of fragile documents and photographs. Check the museum's website for current information.

GREENSBORO LUNCH COUNTER

On February 1, 1960, four African American students sat down at this counter and asked to be served. They remained in their seats even though they were refused service and asked to leave. Their "passive sit-down demand" began the first sustained sit-in and ignited a youth-led movement to challenge injustice and inequality throughout the South. This defiant movement heightened many Americans' awareness of racial injustice and ultimately led to the desegregation of the F. W. Woolworth lunch counter on July 25, 1960.

THIRD FLOOR

THE AMERICAN PRESIDENCY: A GLORIOUS BURDEN

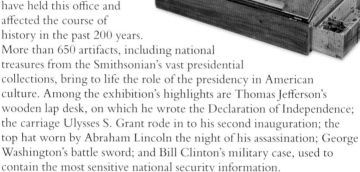

The American Presidency: A Glorious Burden looks at the personal, public, ceremonial, and executive actions of the men who have held this office and affected the course of history in the past 200 years. More than 650 artifacts, including national treasures from the Smithsonian's vast presidential collections, bring to life the role of the presidency in American culture. Among the exhibition's highlights are Thomas Jefferson's wooden lap desk, on which he wrote the Declaration of Independence; the carriage Ulysses S. Grant rode in to his second inauguration; the top hat worn by Abraham Lincoln the night of his assassination; George Washington's battle sword; and Bill Clinton's military case, used to contain the most sensitive national security information.

THE PRICE OF FREEDOM: AMERICANS AT WAR

This 18,000-square-foot exhibition surveys the history of the US military from the colonial era to the present, exploring ways that wars have been defining episodes in American history. Using a unique blend of more than 800 original artifacts, graphic images, and interactive stations, the

ABOVE: Thomas Jefferson drafted the Declaration of Independence on this portable desk from 1865.

LEFT: Abraham Lincoln wore this suit, comprising a black broadcloth coat, trousers, and vest, during his presidency. The hat is the one he wore to Ford's Theatre the night of his assassination.

OPPOSITE: The Continental fleet's gunboat *Philadelphia*, which sank in battle in 1776, was discovered in and raised from Lake Champlain in 1935.

exhibition tells the story of how Americans have fought to establish the nation's independence, determine its borders, shape its values of freedom and opportunity, and define its leading role in world affairs. Among the objects included in the exhibition are one of the few Revolutionary War uniforms in existence; furniture used by Generals Ulysses S. Grant and Robert E. Lee during the surrender ceremony at Appomattox Court House; a restored "Huey" helicopter, an icon of the Vietnam War and the largest object on display; and the uniform Colin Powell wore during Operation Desert Storm.

GUNBOAT *PHILADELPHIA*

In October 1776, American troops in a ragtag collection of newly built boats faced an advancing line of British ships on Lake Champlain in New York. The Americans, under the command of Benedict Arnold, were forced to retreat, but not before they fought the British to a standstill. One of the American vessels, *Philadelphia*, sank during the battle and rested on the bottom of the lake until 1935. It was recovered that year with much of its equipment intact, and came to the museum in 1964, complete with the 24-pound ball that had sent the gunboat to the bottom. This exhibition may close in late 2020 or early 2021 for conservation. Check americanhistory. si.edu for details.

THE FIRST LADIES

The First Ladies explores the unofficial but important position of the first lady and the ways different women have shaped the role to make contributions to the presidential administrations and the nation. The exhibition features more than two dozen gowns from the Smithsonian's almost 100-year-old First Ladies Collection, including those worn by Frances Cleveland, Lou Hoover, Jacqueline Kennedy, Laura Bush, and Michelle Obama. A section titled "Changing Times, Changing First Ladies" highlights the interests and responsibilities of Dolley Madison, Mary Lincoln, Edith Roosevelt, and Lady Bird Johnson and their achievements during their husbands' administrations. *The First Ladies* encourages visitors to consider the changing roles played by the first ladies and American women over the past 200 years.

NICHOLAS F. AND EUGENIA TAUBMAN HALL OF MUSIC

The Hall of Music is the home of the Smithsonian Chamber Music Society. Check the museum's website for concert schedules.

LEFT: Antonio Stradivari (c. 1644–1737) of Cremona, Italy, crafted a number of decorated string instruments that are now in the museum's collection, including those known as the Ole Bull, a violin made in 1687, the Greffuhle violin from 1709, the Axelrod viola built in 1695, and the Marylebone cello of 1688.

BELOW: Dresses worn by the first ladies, including Mary Todd Lincoln and Dolley Madison, are on display in *The First Ladies*.

RUBY SLIPPERS AND AMERICAN CULTURE

Dorothy's ruby slippers are on view as one of eight installations displaying American history through culture, entertainment, and the arts. Other artifacts on view include the New York Yankee Stadium ticket booth, jazz and classical instruments, a video game wall, and cases for new acquisitions. A stained-glass window from the Victor Company's headquarters in Camden, New Jersey, featuring Nipper, the iconic dog listening to his master's recorded voice, is the culture floor's landmark object.

LOWER LEVEL: TAKING AMERICA TO LUNCH

Taking America to Lunch celebrates the history of American lunch boxes. After lunch boxes reached the height of their popularity at the dawn of the television era, lunch box sales became barometers for what was hip in popular culture at any point in time. Included in the display are approximately 75 objects drawn from the museum's collection of children's and workers' illustrated metal lunch boxes and beverage containers dating from the 1880s through the 1980s.

ABOVE: This steel lunch box was manufactured by Aladdin Industries in 1971 and features images from the television show *Woody Woodpecker*.

BELOW: These ruby slippers were made famous by Dorothy Gale, a character portrayed by Judy Garland (1922–1969), in the 1939 film *The Wizard of Oz*.

OPPOSITE: The flag that inspired the national anthem is displayed at the heart of the museum in a specially constructed gallery.

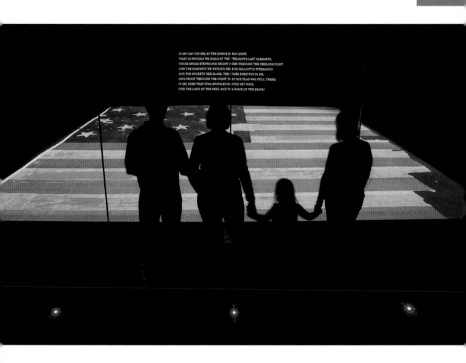

GENERAL INFORMATION

INFORMATION SERVICES
For information and maps, visit the Welcome Center on the second floor or the information desk on the first floor. Information is also available online at americanhistory.si.edu.

PUBLIC PROGRAMS, TOURS, AND DEMONSTRATIONS
The museum offers tours and public programs daily. For information about tours, concerts, lectures, living history theater, and more, inquire at the information desk or Welcome Center, call 202-633-1000, or visit the museum's website. For inquiries about school tours, call 202-633-3717 or visit the museum's website.

ACCESSIBILITY
Barrier-free entrances to the National Museum of American History are located on Madison Drive and Constitution Avenue. Assistive listening devices are available upon request for highlights tours and events in the Warner Bros. Theater, the Hall of Music,

Unity Square, and the Performance Plaza. Sign language interpretation of public programs and tours is available upon request. Because the museum does not have interpreters or captioning reporters on staff, two weeks' notice is preferred. Please call 202-633-3717 or email nmahviptours@si.edu.

DINING
The Eat at America's Table Café is the main eatery for the National Museum of American History. This newly renovated café serves a changing menu of American regional cuisine on the lower level. In the LeRoy Neiman Jazz Café on the first floor, visitors can enjoy light fare, espresso, hand-dipped ice cream, and a view onto bustling Constitution Avenue.

SHOPPING
Museum stores located on the first and second floors offer a wide variety of objects and publications relating to American history, plus postcards, T-shirts, posters, and more.

NATIONAL MUSEUM OF AFRICAN AMERICAN HISTORY AND CULTURE

The National Museum of African American History and Culture is the only national museum devoted exclusively to the documentation of African American life, history, and culture. To date, the museum has collected more than 37,000 artifacts. Visitors can learn about African American history and culture through exhibits focusing on topics such as slavery, the Civil War, the Civil Rights Movement, music, media, and politics.

OPPOSITE: The National Museum of African American History and Culture is on the National Mall, seen here from the north side, with the Washington Monument in the background.

1400 Constitution Avenue NW

(between the Washington Monument and National Museum of American History)

Mall entrance: between 14th and 15th Streets NW

Open daily from 10 a.m. to 5:30 p.m. Closed December 25

Metrorail: Federal Triangle or Smithsonian station

Smithsonian information: 202-633-1000
Museum information: 202-633-4751
nmaahc.si.edu

A PEOPLE'S JOURNEY, A NATION'S STORY

The journey to build the National Museum of African American History and Culture took more than 100 years and numerous steps to realization, including the passage of federal legislation, construction of a majestic new building, and the collection of thousands of artifacts and works of art. It involved the efforts of presidents and members of Congress, curators and architects, art collectors and army veterans, and countless other American citizens.

At the heart of the museum's mission are the collections, providing a tangible connection to the past and evoking the people, places, moments, and ideas that have defined and shaped the African American experience. Unlike many museums, the National Museum of African American History and Culture was not founded on an existing collection. In order to tell the stories it was created to tell, the museum had to seek out and acquire objects that would bring these stories to life.

Since 2005 the museum has collected more than 37,000 artifacts, some 3,000 of which are on display in the exhibition galleries. Many of

BELOW: In Heritage Hall, looking east toward the Walmart Welcome Center (left) and the Robert Frederick Smith Family Corona Pavilion (center). Richard Hunt's sculpture, *Swing Low*, hangs from the ceiling.

these objects have been acquired through the generosity of individuals, families, and organizations who offered their treasured possessions and heirlooms as gifts to the nation. The museum's collection encompasses a wide range of object types, from fine art and photography to manuscripts, musical instruments, clothing and textiles, tools and equipment, and other memorabilia. Artifacts also range widely in size, from hatpins, coins, and campaign buttons to a railroad passenger car, a biplane, a Cadillac, and a log cabin.

The museum presents the story of the United States through an African American lens. This mission, to provide a new perspective on the national experience, is embedded in the form of the building itself. Rising between the Washington Monument and the National Museum of American History, the museum stands alongside the other grand structures on the National Mall, in harmony with its monumental surroundings. But its striking design, defined by the bronze-colored, three-tiered corona, also announces a distinctive presence: independent, proud, resilient, and triumphant. Just as the building has shifted and reshaped the view of the national landscape, it promises a transformative experience for visitors.

FIRST FLOOR
HERITAGE HALL
Both main entrances, on the north and south sides of the museum, open onto Heritage Hall. Spanning the entire ground floor, offering sweeping views in all directions through its glass walls, this welcoming entry space is both grand and intimate.

The interior views of Heritage Hall are equally stunning, with works of contemporary art by Chakaia Booker (*The Liquidity of Legacy*, 2016) and Sam Gilliam (*Yet Do I Marvel,* 2016) adorning the walls and a dramatic, welded-bronze sculpture by Richard Hunt (*Swing Low*, 2016) suspended from the ceiling.

Near the escalators is the Walmart Welcome Center, where visitors can pick up maps and get information about daily programs and tours. The Robert Frederick Smith Family Corona Pavilion, a 60-seat theater, offers regular showings of two short films, *August 28: A Day in the Life of a People* by Ava DuVernay, and *Creating a National Museum*. The museum store is also located on this level.

CONCOURSE
CONTEMPLATIVE COURT
The Concourse level is where visitors enter the David M. Rubenstein History Galleries—three exhibitions that chronicle the African American experience over the course of 600 years of history. Adjacent to the entrance to the History Galleries is the Contemplative Court, one of the signature spaces of the museum. Centered around a waterfall that cascades down from a circular skylight, enclosed by amber-colored glass walls that glow like a beacon above the History Galleries, the Contemplative Court offers a place to sit, reflect, and recharge.

OPRAH WINFREY THEATER

Across from the History Galleries and the Contemplative Court is the entrance to the Oprah Winfrey Theater, a state-of-the-art, 350-seat auditorium that offers film screenings, theatrical performances, lectures, and other public programs.

SPECIAL EXHIBITIONS GALLERY

A large special exhibitions gallery is also located on the Concourse level, featuring temporary exhibitions on various topics related to African American history and culture.

DINING

The Concourse is also where visitors will find Sweet Home Café, the museum's spectacular homage to African American food traditions. Serving stations offer cuisines from different American regions, including the Northern States, the Agricultural South, the Creole Coast, and the Western Range. In the seating area, exhibits along the wall explore the history and culture of African American foodways.

ABOVE: The Contemplative Court is located on the Concourse level.

LEFT: Sweet Home Café, which has seating for 400, welcomes visitors for lunch daily from 11 a.m. to 3 p.m.

THE DAVID M. RUBENSTEIN HISTORY GALLERIES

Literally and symbolically, the History Galleries serve as the foundation upon which the National Museum of African American History and Culture stands. The entrance to the History Galleries is located on the Concourse level. A large observation window overlooks the monumental, 60-foot-high space, in which three exhibitions, layered one atop another and connected by a series of ramps, traverse through 600 years of history. To start the journey, the visitor takes the large glass elevator down to *Slavery and Freedom*, located on the lowest level of the History Galleries.

SLAVERY AND FREEDOM: 1400–1877

Five hundred years ago, the emergence of the transatlantic slave trade transformed Africa, Europe, and the Americas. People treated other human beings as commodities—things to be bought, sold, and exploited to make enormous profits. This system changed the world.

The United States was created in this context, forged by slavery as well as a radical new concept—freedom. *Slavery and Freedom* explores

LEFT: This handmade tin contains a certificate of freedom issued to Joseph Trammell, Loudoun County, Virginia, 1852.

BELOW: The paradox of liberty: Thomas Jefferson, who declared "all men are created equal," also owned 609 slaves during his lifetime.

ABOVE: Peter Bentzon, a free black artisan in Philadelphia, made this silver teapot, c. 1817–1829.

BELOW: The 150-year-old Point of Pines cabin was carefully dismantled, piece by piece, brought to the museum, and reassembled in the exhibition.

the complexity of this story, which rests at the core of Americans' shared history. Through powerful objects and first-person accounts, it examines slavery from the perspectives of those who experienced it—the enslaved and the enslavers, those who supported and profited from the system, and those who fought to abolish it. As the exhibition considers the central role that slavery played in the origins of the United States, it also reveals the ways in which the actions of ordinary men and women, demanding freedom, transformed the nation.

Slavery and Freedom covers 400 years of history, from the rise of the global slave trade to the founding of the United States and to the Civil War and Reconstruction.

LANDMARK OBJECT: POINT OF PINES CABIN

One of the most significant artifacts in the *Slavery and Freedom* exhibition is a slave cabin from the Point of Pines Plantation on Edisto Island, South Carolina. Built around 1853, likely by enslaved carpenters, the cabin was home to a family who used it to raise children, nurture one another, and build community.

DEFENDING FREEDOM, DEFINING FREEDOM: THE ERA OF SEGREGATION, 1877–1968

The years after the Civil War were both hopeful and disheartening for African Americans. With the end of slavery, they had hoped to attain full citizenship. Instead they found themselves resisting efforts to put in place a new form of oppression—segregation. In the face of these attacks, African Americans created institutions and communities to help them survive and thrive. Through their struggle they challenged the nation to live up to its ideals of freedom and equality.

Defending Freedom, Defining Freedom: The Era of Segregation spans the period from the end of Reconstruction through the modern Civil Rights movement. As visitors make their way through the exhibition, they encounter powerful artifacts that testify to the pressures and threats that African Americans confronted during this era, the strength and resilience of African American communities, and the strategies that civil rights activists employed to effect change.

ABOVE: A biplane flown by Tuskegee Airmen during combat training soars over the ramp leading from the *Era of Segregation* landing theater.

BELOW LEFT: This fragment came from a stained-glass window shattered by the 1963 bombing of 16th Street Baptist Church in Birmingham, Alabama.

BELOW: Activist Rosa Parks made this dress in 1955–1956. Her arrest in 1955 for defying segregation laws sparked the Montgomery bus boycott.

ABOVE: Shown is one of the lunch counter stools used in the Woolworth's sit-in, Greensboro, North Carolina, 1960.

BELOW: At the interactive lunch counter, visitors explore how civil rights activists brought about social change.

INTERACTIVE LUNCH COUNTER

In a large space at the center of the exhibition, an interactive lunch counter puts you into the shoes—and onto the stools—of civil rights activists to understand how their individual choices and collective actions changed history. Here the visitor can explore scenarios drawn from real events of the Civil Rights Movement and consider what choices they would have made or actions they would have taken in those situations.

LANDMARK OBJECT: SOUTHERN RAILWAY NO. 1200

Across from the interactive lunch counter, a segregated railroad passenger car offers visitors a firsthand encounter with the separate and unequal conditions that African Americans experienced while living and traveling under Jim Crow. During the 1940s, the Southern Railway Company operated a long-distance passenger service between Washington, DC, and New Orleans. To comply with state laws that required public transportation to be segregated, the company outfitted this coach with a partition to create separate seating sections for white and black passengers. The coach, now restored to its 1940s condition, is open for visitors to step inside and walk through.

ABOVE: A segregated railroad car of the Southern Railway Company illustrates the separate—and unequal—conditions that black travelers experienced during Jim Crow.

TOP: "Black is Beautiful" was a cultural movement in the 1960s and 1970s that referred to a broad embrace of black culture and identity.

ABOVE LEFT: This placard was carried during the April 8, 1968, memorial march in Memphis following the assassination of Martin Luther King Jr.

ABOVE RIGHT: Shirley Chisholm was the first black woman elected to Congress and, in 1972, the first to run for president.

OPPOSITE: Through education, faith, and other community institutions, African Americans forged possibilities in a world that denied them opportunities.

A CHANGING AMERICA: 1968 AND BEYOND

Over the past 50 years, African Americans have continued to seek racial equality and social justice. As with previous generations, this contemporary quest for freedom has been marked both by progress and paradox, breakthroughs and backlash. *A Changing America: 1968 and Beyond*, located on the top level of the History Galleries, explores social, political, and cultural changes in American society from the death of Martin Luther King Jr. into the 21st century. It examines the strategies African Americans have used to wrestle with racial discrimination, cultural exclusion, and economic inequality and considers how issues of immigration, class, and gender have reshaped the definition of African American identity at the turn of the present century.

THE BLACK POWER ERA

The centerpiece of *A Changing America* is a dynamic multimedia presentation that immerses the visitor in the politics and culture of the Black Power era. Scenes and sounds from the turbulent year of 1968 play on a central overhead screen, while nine displays shaped like picket signs fan out through the space and explore the assassination of Martin Luther King Jr., religion and Black Power, the Black Panther Party, the Vietnam War, electoral politics, the Black Arts Movement, black feminism, film and television, and black middle-class consciousness.

COMMUNITY GALLERIES:
THIRD FLOOR

A sense of community—forged by shared experiences, nurtured through organizations and institutions, and expressed through values of service, mutual assistance, and uplift—has been a core component of African American life and a key to surviving racial oppression. On the third floor of the museum, exhibitions explore different ways in which African Americans have created and cultivated this sense of community. As African Americans organized for mutual benefit and support, participated in sports and military service, and built places to live, learn, work, worship, and play, they also carved out spaces for pursuing political goals and effecting social change.

MAKING A WAY OUT OF NO WAY

Taking its title from a popular African American expression, *Making a Way Out of No Way* explores different strategies that black communities have used for survival and support and to effect social change. At the entrance, a multiscreen media wall and iconic artifacts introduce the major topics of the exhibition. The exhibition continues down the halls on either side of the media wall, encircling the Community floor. Each section is organized around a central theme: faith, education, organizations, enterprise, the press, and activism.

BLACK-OWNED BUSINESSES

The National Baptist Publishing Board, founded by R. H. Boyd in 1896, supplied publications and other materials for black churches and served as a hub for black business development in Nashville. Known today as the R. H. Boyd Publishing Corporation, it is one of the oldest continuously operated, family-run African American businesses. This time clock, manufactured around 1912, was used by workers at the company's Nashville plant.

POWER OF PLACE

In *Power of Place*, visitors can explore stories of place from across the wide expanse of the nation and the African American experience. A sense of place has deeply shaped African American communities, forming and changing identities in all corners of the country and in turn influencing the regions around them. Their evolution reveals a set of stories as varied as the landscape itself. Featured places include Lyles Station, a farming community in Indiana; Oak Bluffs, a resort on Martha's Vineyard, Massachusetts; Louisiana's Angola prison; the Bronx, New York; and Mae Reeves's hat shop in Philadelphia.

LEFT: This workers' time clock was used at the National Baptist Publishing Board plant, Nashville, c. 1912.

BOTTOM LEFT: Mae Reeves's millinery shop in Philadelphia was a place of civic engagement and racial integration, and her hats were works of art.

BOTTOM RIGHT: By creating spaces for diverse youth cultures and musical styles to mix, exchange, and innovate, the Bronx became the birthplace of hip-hop.

THE HOMETOWN HUB

At the Hometown Hub, personal stories shared through an interactive table reveal connections between place and memory, community, and identity. The Hometown Hub interactive is located at the center of the *Power of Place* exhibition.

DOUBLE VICTORY:
THE AFRICAN AMERICAN MILITARY EXPERIENCE

Double Victory: The African American Military Experience explores the history of African Americans in the military and the impact of their contributions, both within the military and in the broader society. In 1942 the *Pittsburgh Courier,* an African American newspaper, launched the Double Victory

Campaign to rally patriotic support during World War II. This fight for a "Double Victory"—against enemies abroad and racism as home—has reverberated throughout the long history of the African American military experience, from the colonial era to the War on Terror.

THE MEDAL OF HONOR GALLERY

The Medal of Honor gallery features the stories of those who epitomized their nation's call for selfless service and the medal's requirements for "gallantry" and "actions above and beyond the call of duty." The gallery highlights each African American who has received the Medal of Honor and features the medal awarded posthumously to Sgt. Cornelius H. Charlton, who was killed in action while leading an assault on enemy forces during the Korean War. Sergeant Charlton is one of several African American Medal of Honor recipients buried in Arlington National Cemetery, which can be viewed in the distance through a window at the end of the gallery.

OPPOSITE TOP: Visitors interact with the Hometown Hub in the *Power of Place* exhibition.

OPPOSITE BOTTOM LEFT: An ambrotype of Sgt. Qualls Tibbs, 27th USCT, Camp Delaware, Ohio, 1864-1865.

OPPOSITE BOTTOM RIGHT: A patriotic "Double V" handkerchief (1942-1945) symbolizes the battle against racial discrimination on the home front during World War II.

BELOW: The gallery dedicated to African American Medal of Honor recipients offers a dramatic view of the Washington Monument.

SPORTS: LEVELING THE PLAYING FIELD

Sports: Leveling the Playing Field explores the role of sports as a vehicle for African American athletic performance, cultural expression, and political activism. Sports matter far beyond the playing field. Historically, African American athletes were denied opportunities to compete at the highest levels. Yet as one of the earliest public arenas to accept African Americans on terms of relative equality, sports have also served as a measuring stick for racial progress. Beyond the impressive records of individual achievements, the history of sports also demonstrates how African Americans have used sports to fight for greater rights and freedoms.

Special sections in *Sports: Leveling the Playing Field* focus on major sports and events, including football, baseball, the Olympics, boxing, and basketball. Stories of the "Game Changers" examine the impact of individual athletes and athletic institutions on sports, culture, and society.

ABOVE: Muhammad Ali wore this boxing headgear c. 1973.

BELOW: Althea Gibson, the first African American to win a Grand Slam title, used this tennis racket c. 1960.

BOTTOM: When African American athletes protested against racism at the 1968 Olympics, they demonstrated the impact of sports beyond the playing field.

CULTURE GALLERIES: FOURTH FLOOR

African American culture has served as a tool for survival, a focus for creativity, a source of identity, and a force for change. Forged from traditions shared with other people of the African diaspora, it has evolved through innovation, improvisation, and exchange and has embraced many different forms. The fourth floor of the museum is dedicated to exploring the wide spectrum of African American culture, from music, performing arts, painting, and sculpture to language, fashion, and food.

CULTURAL EXPRESSIONS

As visitors arrive on the museum's fourth floor, *Cultural Expressions* surrounds them with the vibrant sights, sounds, and textures of African American culture. Exhibition sections, arranged in a colorful patchwork of curved cases, explore five different forms of African American cultural expression: style, movement, foodways, artistry, and language. The central space, the Cultural Commons, examines cultural connections between African Americans and other people of the African diaspora. Overhead, a 360-degree media projection presents a kaleidoscope of images, music, and words that evoke the richness and diversity of African American culture.

The exhibition also features a bottle tree, created by contemporary artist Stephanie Dwyer in homage to a traditional practice brought to the American South by enslaved Africans, and a rotating display of quilts from the museum's collection that reflect the diversity of African American quilting traditions, patterns, and styles.

ABOVE: A sculpture by Olowe of Ise, a Yoruba artist, is a focal point of the *Cultural Expressions* gallery.

LEFT: The image of Anansi the spider on this Ecuadorean boat seat of the early 1900s evokes storytelling traditions shared across the African diaspora.

MUSICAL CROSSROADS

Musical Crossroads explores the history and culture of African American music through a captivating array of artifacts, images, and sounds, organized by musical styles and related themes. At the entrance, a red Cadillac Eldorado owned by Chuck Berry evokes the sense of freedom, exuberance, and innovation that defined rock and roll. At the center of the gallery, an immersive video features performances by African American musicians across time and genre.

THE P-FUNK MOTHERSHIP

Among the many evocative objects collected by the museum to tell the story of African American music, one literally hovers above the rest. The P-Funk Mothership first appeared on the cover of Parliament's 1975 futuristic concept album, *Mothership Connection*, and continued to appear at performances by George Clinton and his band for the next two decades. A replica of the original Mothership, created for the Mothership Reconnection Tours in the 1990s, was donated to the museum by Clinton in 2011.

TAKING THE STAGE

Taking the Stage explores the history of African Americans on the stage and screen, celebrating their creative achievements, demonstrating their cultural impact, and illuminating their struggles for artistic freedom and equal representation. At the entrance to the gallery, visitors are greeted by a collage of more than 100 portraits of artists and entertainers, reflecting the diversity of African American performance from the 1800s to the present. The exhibition unfolds in three main sections: theater, film, and television.

ABOVE: Spotlights illuminate famous artists of the stage and screen at the entrance to *Taking the Stage*.

RIGHT: The 1922 film *The Crimson Skull*, produced by Norman Studios, featured an all–African American cast.

OPPOSITE TOP: Nona Hendryx of Labelle wore this costume in 1975.

OPPOSITE: Chuck Berry's 1973 Cadillac Eldorado welcomes visitors to the *Musical Crossroads* exhibition.

VISUAL ART AND THE AMERICAN EXPERIENCE

Visual arts play a vital role in illuminating the American experience through an African American lens. Paintings, sculptures, and works on paper offer insight into how artists viewed and interpreted their world. *Visual Art and the American Experience* illustrates the critical role that artists of African descent played in shaping the history of American art. The exhibition is organized into seven thematic sections and also includes a small changing exhibit gallery.

AMY SHERALD, *GRAND DAME QUEENIE*, 2012

Identity—the terms by which we define who we are—is central to the way we navigate our lives, and is also complex and multifaceted. Several artists featured in *Visual Art and the American Experience* have examined the relationship of race to identity. In this enigmatic portrait by Amy Sherald, a young woman sips tea from a cup adorned by the silhouetted head of a black woman. The painting offers a visual commentary on the topic of imposed identity as it relates to the process of role playing and assimilation during the Italian Renaissance and in modern-day society. Amy Sherald's portrait quietly invites the viewer to contemplate a variety of subjects, including race, class, identity, and self-acceptance.

LEFT: Amy Sherald (b. 1973). *Grand Dame Queenie*, 2012. Oil on canvas. © Amy Sherald.

OPPOSITE: Sculpted of wood from President Obama's inauguration platform, Jefferson Pinder's *Mothership (Capsule)*, 2009, center, is in the "New Materials, New Worlds" section.

EXPLORE MORE! SECOND FLOOR

Explore More! is an interactive, multifaceted educational space dedicated to helping visitors connect and engage with African American history and culture in ways that expand perspectives, spark curiosity and creativity, and increase knowledge. Located on the museum's second floor, the space is designed to complement and expand on themes and topics presented in the permanent exhibition galleries on the History, Community, and Culture floors. Through the combined use of multimedia technology, exhibitions and collections, live performance, and hands-on activities, Explore More! offers a dynamic and personalized museum experience for visitors of all ages.

TARGET LEARNING CENTER

At the heart of the Explore More! floor is the Target Learning Center, an interactive gallery with adjoining classrooms. Public programs and hands-on learning activities are also regularly offered in the interactive gallery. The classrooms provide flexible spaces for student and teacher programs, workshops, demonstrations, and other group-learning activities.

INTERACTIVES

Interactive experiences in the Explore More! gallery include the Arc, a 30-foot-long curved digital wall populated with objects and stories from the museum collections. Visitors can also join in a virtual step show, investigate the wreck of a slave ship, and take a cross-country trip using the *Green Book*, a travel guide produced for African Americans during the era of segregation.

ROBERT FREDERICK SMITH
EXPLORE YOUR FAMILY HISTORY CENTER

In the Robert Frederick Smith Explore Your Family History Center, visitors can delve into digital resources related to family history, including the Freedmen's Bureau digital archives and genealogical databases; receive expert guidance on how to conduct genealogical research; view exhibits and objects from the museum's collection relating to family history; and learn how to preserve family photographs, documents, and audiovisual materials.

EARL W. AND AMANDA STAFFORD
CENTER FOR AFRICAN AMERICAN MEDIA ARTS

Located at the entrance to the Explore More! floor, the Earl W. and Amanda Stafford Center for African American Media Arts (CAAMA) is dedicated to examining the formation of African American history and culture through the media arts, including photography, film, video, and audio recordings. In its space—a dramatic red, glass-encased "jewel box"—CAAMA offers a regular schedule of changing exhibitions that showcase historical themes and current trends in the media arts.

LIBRARY AND ARCHIVES

The NMAAHC Research Library and Archives provides access to resources that support scholarship in African American history, culture, and the African diaspora. The library features a reading room with computer stations, stack space for 11,000 volumes, and electronic, print, and archival resources. An exhibit case next to the entrance features rotating displays of library books and archival materials. The library is open to public researchers by appointment.

GENERAL INFORMATION

LOCATION

The National Museum of African American History and Culture is located on the National Mall at 1400 Constitution Avenue NW, between Madison and Constitution Avenues and 14th and 15th Streets NW, Washington, DC. The museum has two entrances, one on Madison Avenue and another on Constitution Avenue.

ADMISSION

Free, but timed passes may be required for entry. Please visit the museum website for more information.

MUSEUM WEBSITE

For information about NMAAHC, including timed-entry passes, directions, current and upcoming exhibitions, special events, and public programs, visit nmaahc.si.edu.

MOBILE APP

The NMAAHC mobile app serves as a complement to the on-site museum experience and a way to discover some of the many stories found in the museum's collection. Features include exhibition highlights tours, stories for families with children, and multimedia and augmented reality experiences, along with maps, program schedules, and other visitor information. Audio stories are available in English, French, and Spanish. The app is free and available to download for iOS and Android devices via the museum website.

PROGRAMS AND TOURS

The museum hosts a robust series of discussions, readings, concerts, screenings, and workshops that highlight our exciting exhibitions and collections for a diverse community of learners. Docent-led tours are also offered on a regular basis. Please visit the museum website for the most current information and program schedule.

LEFT: Interactive experiences in the Explore More! gallery include "Follow the Green Book," about travel during the era of segregation, and the Arc, a digital collections wall.

ACCESSIBILITY OPTIONS

The museum is accessible for visitors with limited mobility via escalators, elevators, and ramps, and manual wheelchairs are available to borrow on a first-come, first-served basis. For visitors who are blind or experience low vision, the museum offers Braille/raised image maps and large print maps, as well as sighted guide and verbal description by trained docents and visitor services staff. All videos in the museum are open captioned. The NMAAHC visitor services team also offers sensory maps and pre-visit planning guides for visitors who have cognitive or sensory processing disabilities. For more information on specific resources and accommodations, visit the museum website or contact the Smithsonian Accessibility Office at www.si.edu/accessibility.

DINING

The Sweet Home Café, located on the Concourse level, seats 400 people, features a rotating menu of seasonal offerings served at four stations, and includes family-friendly options. The stations are organized to showcase traditional African American cuisine from the following US regions: the Northern States, the Agricultural South, the Creole Coast, and the Western Range. Visitors are not allowed to bring food into the museum, and coolers are also not permitted in the museum or on the grounds.

SHOPPING

The main museum store is located in Heritage Hall and offers a wide selection of items reflecting the experience, architecture, and collections of the museum. A pop-up store is also located on Level 3 outside the Community Galleries.

MEMBERSHIP

To become a member of the National Museum of the African American History and Culture and receive exclusive benefits, call 800-209-9178 or visit nmaahc.si.edu/give.

Judy Davis/Hoachlander Davis Photography, ©2004

Photo by David Heald

NATIONAL MUSEUM OF THE AMERICAN INDIAN

The National Museum of the American Indian (NMAI) is an institution of living cultures, featuring the lifeways, history, and art of Indigenous peoples throughout the Western Hemisphere. The museum is housed in two public facilities: the National Museum of the American Indian on the National Mall in Washington, DC, and the George Gustav Heye Center in New York City. The Cultural Resources Center in Suitland, Maryland, is open by appointment only.

OPPOSITE: NMAI Director Kevin Gover helps fifth-grade students from New York City Public School 276 build bridges during the imagiNATIONS Activity Center grand opening. (Jason DeCrow/AP Images for NMAI)

In Washington, DC:
Fourth Street and Independence Ave SW
Open daily from 10 a.m. to 5:30 p.m.
Closed December 25
Metrorail: L'Enfant Plaza station
Smithsonian information: 202-633-1000
AmericanIndian.si.edu

In New York City:
One Bowling Green
Open 10 a.m. to 5:00 p.m.; Thursdays until 8 p.m. Closed December 25
Subway: Bowling Green station
212-514-3700

In Suitland, MD:
Cultural Resources Center
4220 Silver Hill Road
301-238-1435

A NEW KIND OF MEETING PLACE

For Native peoples, the existential challenges that come from misrepresentation are real, and efforts to counteract them never cease. For non-Native peoples, the loss that comes from misrepresentation is real as well—beginning with a failure to acknowledge and connect. With this understanding, a persistent group of visionaries, activists, legislators, and community leaders set out to establish a museum that could be a force for equity and social justice for the peoples of the Western Hemisphere. To be that force, in partnership with Native peoples and their allies, the National Museum of the American Indian fosters a richer shared human experience through a more informed understanding of Native peoples.

The museum has three branches. The newest branch of the museum is the namesake National Museum of the American Indian, which opened on the National Mall in 2004 and presents a wide range of exhibitions, screenings, presentations, and school and public programs. Designed in consultation with Native people, the sweeping curvilinear building represents the spirit of Native America on the nation's front lawn and symbolizes the enduring presence of Native Americans in contemporary life.

BELOW: Pamela Saleta (center) encourages the audience to join the *moceñada*, a traditional dance of the Andes region in South America honoring La Pachamama (Mother Earth) and offering thanks.

OPPOSITE TOP: Reuben Martinez (Pojoaque) from the Pueblo of Pojoaque's Poeh Cultural Center and Museum discusses loan selections with NMAI assistant director for collections Cynthia Chavez Lamar (San Felipe/Hopi/Tewa/Navajo).

OPPOSITE BELOW: Clockwise from lower left: Storyteller bracelet, ca. 1990. Joseph Coriz (Santo Domingo Pueblo, b. 1958). Bracelet, ca. 1988. Angie Reano Owen (Santo Domingo Pueblo, b. 1946). Bracelet, ca. 1983. Jesse Monongye (Navajo/Hopi, b. 1952).

The museum also has a location in New York City, home of the largest urban population of Native people in the United States. This facility is the direct descendant of the original Museum of the American Indian established in New York by George Gustav Heye, an avid collector of Native American cultural items. Opened in 1916, the museum became part of the Smithsonian in 1989.

Today the greater part of the collection of more than 800,000 objects and 125,000 images is housed in Suitland, Maryland, just outside Washington, DC, in an enormous, nautilus-shaped building known as

the Cultural Resources Center. This facility provides state-of-the-art resources for the conservation, handling, cataloging, and study of the museum's collections, library holdings, and photo and paper archives.

A CALL TO COMMITMENT

A sign placed in the Washington, DC, museum's landscape states, "This is a Native place." As such, in partnership with Indigenous people, the museum works with Native nations to tell more complete and accurate stories and foster a sense of community with and among these nations. The museum is also upending conventions in conservation circles and helping to reverse the centuries of theft of Native art, artifacts, and identity that non-Native institutions have carried out. It is returning much to its rightful owners; approximately one-third of the original collection has now been repatriated.

The museum's staff now reinterprets the collections with both academic discipline and traditional knowledge. Pueblo potters not only add to the museum's knowledge of an object's history and how it was made; they also open conservators' eyes to the importance of preserving evidence of its use—soot on a cooking pot, for example—so that visitors can better understand its value in the life of a family or community.

CHANGING PRACTICES AND PERCEPTIONS

On every floor of the museum, tribal flags are presented in various ways; visitors of all backgrounds are struck by the flags' vividness and variety. Visitors from Native nations look to see if the flag of their own nation is displayed among them. For Native people, the flags represent the independence, or sovereignty, of each tribal nation and the importance of respecting this unique status; this concept is reinforced throughout the museum's exhibitions.

The cornerstone exhibition in Washington, DC, *Americans,* can lead to revelation. It presents many of the most pervasive images and stories of Indians in the United States and deconstructs them with a keen, critical, and at times humorous eye.

American Indian images, names, and stories infuse American history and contemporary life. The images are everywhere, from the names of products to sports mascots, and from classic Westerns and cartoons to episodes of *Seinfeld* and *South Park.* American Indian names are everywhere too, from state, city, and street names to the Tomahawk missile. And the familiar historical events of Pocahontas's life, the Trail of Tears, and the Battle of Little Bighorn remain popular reference points in everyday conversations. The *Americans* gallery features these images and hundreds more, highlighting the ways in which American Indians have been part of the nation's identity since before the country began. It surrounds visitors with images, delves into the three historical stories, and invites them to begin a conversation about why this phenomenon exists.

Pervasive, powerful, at times demeaning, these images, names, and stories reveal the deep connection between Americans and American Indians as well as how Indians have been

OPPOSITE: In the large, sunlit Potomac Atrium of the Washington museum, the flags of dozens of Native nations hang in a sweeping arc.

BELOW: The *Americans* exhibition features nearly 350 objects and images in a striking floor-to-ceiling assembly, all showing that Indian names and images are everywhere in American life. Photo by Thomas Loof for Studio Joseph.

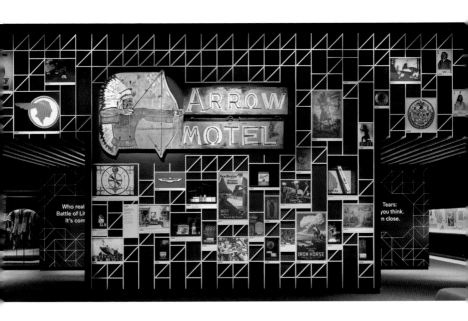

embedded in unexpected ways in the history, pop culture, and identity of the United States. In pushing past the stereotypes, *Americans* is likely to leave visitors with at least two powerful impressions: how pervasive Indian images and stereotypes truly are in the popular culture and everyday life of the United States, and how much more interesting—fascinating, even—the real stories turn out to be.

In Washington, the museum's major exhibition *Nation to Nation: Treaties Between the United States and American Indian Nations* shines a light on treaties and does more than deepen an understanding of history. Each treaty on display, on loan from the National Archives, is a living document that informs legal battles about land and other Native rights that continue to make headlines today.

Near the entrance of the *Nation to Nation* exhibition stands a landmark, 2,200-pound tableau, *Allies in War, Partners in Peace,* a gift from the Oneida Indian Nation of New York. Originally presented to the museum in 2004, it commemorates the aid the Oneida people gave to George Washington and his struggling Continental army during the early days of the American Revolution. The sculpture features an interpretive surround, enhancing the storytelling of the piece itself with light, sound, and projected imagery.

Honoring the military service of Native people since the colonial era is a theme throughout the museum. An exhibition and short film in the second-level Sealaska Gallery, *Why We Serve: Native Americans in the United States Armed Forces*, offer compelling stories and first-person accounts of both war and peacetime service.

Opened in fall 2020, the museum fulfilled its charge from Congress to establish a National Native American Veterans Memorial to give "all Americans the opportunity to learn of the proud

"This is still our land, and it's our nature to protect our land ... our lives, and our children, and the people around us."

—HARVEY PRATT

OPPOSITE: Hundreds of handmade signs were nailed to this mile-marker post by activists at the Dakota Access Pipeline protest site. The signs point toward protestors' cities, states, American Indian Nations, or countries.

BELOW: Designed by Marine Corps Vietnam veteran Harvey Pratt (Cheyenne/Arapaho), the National Native American Veterans Memorial honors the commitment and bravery of American Indian, Alaska Native, and Native Hawaiian members of the US Armed Forces. Design by Harvey Pratt/Butzer Architects and Urbanism. Alan Karchmer for NMAI.

and courageous tradition of service of Native Americans in the armed forces of the United States." This tribute to Native heroes, positioned in the northeast portion of the museum's landscape within sight of the US Capitol, honors Native Americans in every branch of the US Armed Forces and ensures that their legacy of enduring and distinguished service at last receives the national recognition it deserves.

To highlight the creative work of talented Native Americans in film and offer the public insight into contemporary issues and ways of life in Native communities, the museum screens feature films, documentaries, experimental films, and short works by Indigenous and independent filmmakers. Fictional films shown by the museum represent multiple filmmaking styles and tell diverse Native stories. Documentary programs focus on important themes such as climate change, land rights and sovereignty, and the preservation of Indigenous language and cultural traditions.

With these and other initiatives, NMAI and its partners are beginning to achieve the transformation they seek. They are deepening awareness, convening conversations, and bringing to light the everyday lives and exceptional achievements of Native peoples in ways that enrich every individual who accepts the invitation to enter a Native place.

COLLECTIONS

The collections of the former Museum of the American Indian, Heye Foundation, are the cornerstone of NMAI. Assembled largely by wealthy New Yorker George Gustav Heye (1874–1957), the collections span more than 10,000 years of Native heritage in the United States (including Hawai'i), Canada, and Latin America. Among the thousands of masterworks are intricate wood, horn, and stone carvings from the North Pacific Coast of North America; elegantly painted hides and garments from the Great Plains; pottery and basketry from the southwestern United States; ceramic figures from the Caribbean; jade carved by the Olmec and Maya peoples; textiles and gold offerings made by Andean cultures; elaborate featherwork by the peoples of Amazonia; and paintings and other works by contemporary Native American

BELOW: The angles of solstices and equinoxes are mapped on the Potomac's floor, and a light spectrum is cast across the space by the sun shining through prisms.

artists. About 70 percent of the 800,000 objects represent cultures in Mexico and Central and South America.

The museum on the National Mall was designed by Douglas Cardinal (Blackfoot) and a team of Native architects and consultants to blend into the Mall's urban yet parklike setting while retaining Native values. Natural features of the land, as well as the stone and masonry work of Chaco Canyon, Machu Picchu, and other Native sites, inspired the museum's designers to create a structure in which nature's rugged beauty and architecture's creative elegance come together in perfect harmony. The five-story, 250,000-square-foot curvilinear building, clad in Kasota limestone from Minnesota, evokes a natural rock formation swept by wind and water. Its dome, representative of the circular shapes in many Native cultures, complements the neoclassical buildings nearby.

The museum's entrance on the National Mall faces east toward the rising sun. Just beyond the entrance extends the Potomac Atrium, a circular gathering place for music, dance, cultural events, and tours. The Potomac—from an Algonquian-Powhatan word meaning "where the goods are brought in"—features a 120-foot-high atrium and eight large prism windows that, on sunny days, project a palette of brilliant rainbow colors throughout the space.

The museum has several locations for Native presentations, drama, dance, music performances, demonstrations, readings, and symposia, including the 300-seat Rasmuson Theater (Level 1). The Lelawi Theater (Level 4) presents Who We Are, a 13-minute film that celebrates the vitality and diversity of Native life.

Exhibitions on the second, third, and fourth levels can be accessed from elevators located in the Potomac space. At the imagiNATIONS Activity Center (Level 3), families and young visitors will find an interactive area filled with numerous unique learning experiences.

In New York the museum also presents diverse exhibitions ranging from explorations of historical materials to selections from its vast collections to contemporary art installations. One of the largest galleries features *Infinity of Nations: History and Art in the Collections of the National Museum of the American Indian*, a major exhibition that showcases the cultural, historical, and geographic scope of the museum's holdings.

Inspired by Native works, the Diker Pavilion for Native Arts and Cultures serves as a center for Native art and performance, an education facility for schoolchildren, and a gathering place for the local community. On view in this gallery and performance space is *Ancestral Connections*, which explores how ten contemporary artists draw on aspects of their heritage—sometimes combined with personal experiences or tribal history—to create new and compelling works of art.

LEFT: Shuar Akitai.
Ear ornaments, ca. 1930.
Upper Amazon, Ecuador.

HONORING WOMEN AS STRONG AS BISON HORN

Lakota artists Kevin and Valerie Pourier's concha belt, *Winyan Wánakikśin* (Women Defenders of Others), portrays Native leaders, but it is also a tribute to the strength of all women, represented by the hands of many colors cradling the Earth. The tipis' frames are "like backbones," says Kevin Pourier, "because women are the backbones of the people."

The collective power of these women and the compelling beauty of the piece struck NMAI Director Kevin Gover when he saw the belt displayed at the Santa Fe Indian Market in August 2018. It won Best in Show, and from the moment he saw it, Gover knew that the museum's collection needed this artwork. "I couldn't think of a better piece to—in a very different way—honor the role of women in our country."

The belt's placement in the museum, visible soon after visitors walk in, is no accident. To support the Smithsonian American Women's History Initiative, Gover is bringing women's stories to the forefront: "We need to help add to the narrative about contemporary Native women."

Gover hopes that visitors will note that the portraits are carved into bull bison horn—a remarkable feat. "I can't imagine a more difficult material to work with," he says. Working with this medium is important to the Pouriers. Their studio and home are on the Oglala Lakota's Pine Ridge Indian Reservation in southwest South Dakota, and bison are central to the lives of the Lakota people, from subsistence to ceremonies.

To create the *Winyan Wánakikśin* belt, the conchae were inlaid with a variety of natural materials—pieces of sandstone from South Dakota's Badlands, turquoise, green malachite, deep blue lapis lazuli, pink coral, and the shimmery mother-of-pearl interiors and gold lips of shells—all crushed and mixed with resin to hold the small pieces in place.

GENERAL INFORMATION

INFORMATION DESKS

Visitor and membership information can be obtained at the Welcome Desk on the first level in Washington, DC, and at the New York museum's Information Desk, located in the Great Hall, second floor.

ACCESSIBILITY

Washington, DC
Wheelchairs are available on a first-come, first-served basis. The Aira app is available free of charge in the building on the National Mall for sight-impaired visitors. Visitors can request sign language tours with three weeks' advance notice. See AmericanIndian. si.edu/visit/washington/accessibility for more information.

New York
All exhibitions are wheelchair accessible. Wheelchairs are available free of charge on the ground floor of the museum and may be obtained on request from the security staff. Additional accessibility services can be provided at no cost, with two weeks' advance notice.

EDUCATIONAL PROGRAMS

The museum offers guided and self-guided experiences for students and general visitors to learn about the rich, complex, and dynamic histories and cultures of Indigenous peoples of the Western Hemisphere. Visit AmericanIndian.si.edu for more information.

MEMBERSHIP

To become a member of the National Museum of the American Indian and receive its full-color quarterly magazine, *American Indian*, call 800-242-NMAI (6624) or visit AmericanIndian.si.edu.

IMAGINATIONS ACTIVITY CENTER

Native people are the original innovators of the Americas. This is the powerful message of the imagiNATIONS Activity Center at the museum's two locations. Through the centers' hands-on activities, visitors can explore amazing Native scientific discoveries and inventions that continue to affect the world today. For hours and information, visit AmericanIndian.si.edu.

DINING

Washington, DC
"Mitsitam" means "Let's eat!" in the language of the Delaware peoples. The museum's Mitsitam Native Foods Cafe offers visitors the opportunity to enjoy Native-inspired cuisines of the Americas and to explore the history of Indigenous foods. It features Native foods found throughout the Western Hemisphere. Each of the five food stations—Oceans, Sea, and Streams; Mountains and Plains; the Three Sisters; Contemporary Native; and Native Comfort—depict regional lifeways related to cooking techniques, ingredients, and flavors found in both traditional and contemporary dishes. Selections include authentic Native foods, such as traditional fry bread, as well as contemporary items with a Native American twist.

Mitsitam Espresso Coffee Bar
The museum's Mitsitam Espresso Coffee Bar serves pastries and casual fare from the Mitsitam Cafe's menu. Tables in the coffee bar are adjacent to the Potomac Atrium, the heart of the museum and site of many cultural presentations and festivals.

New York
The Mili Kàpi Cafe offers hot and cold beverages and light casual fare—sandwiches, salads, and sweets—highlighting ingredients indigenous to the Americas. The cafe is located on the second floor, on the same level as the Museum Store. *Mili Kàpi* means "give me some coffee" in the language of the Lenape people, the original inhabitants of New York City.

SHOPPING

Washington, DC
Architecturally warm and inviting,
the Roanoke Museum Store presents
Native American items from the past
and present, illustrating how different
artists interpret cultural traditions and art
forms. On the museum's second level,
the store features jewelry, textiles, and
other works by Native artisans; souvenirs;
and children's books and toys. The name
Roanoke is a reference to the shells once
used as currency by local Native peoples
and reflects the importance of waterways
to Native commerce.

New York
For more than 20 years, the NMAI
Museum Store has served as New York
City's premier destination to purchase
authentic Native American merchandise.
Recently expanded, the store now
features more items from a wider
representation of Native groups than ever
before, offering apparel, art, literature,
jewelry, food, and more for all ages.

The site of the Museum Store historically
served as the cashier's office of the
Alexander Hamilton US Custom House,
which is now a city landmark. In the
early 20th century, revenue from the
Custom House served as one of the
largest funding sources for the federal
government. The renovation of the space
preserves original details like antique
metal dividers for the cashiers' cages,
and design flourishes such as intricate
crown molding, grand chandeliers, and
the original vault used by the cashiers.

In both locations, members of the
museum receive a 10 percent discount
for purchases made at the store;
nonmembers may purchase memberships
onsite to receive the discount.

RIGHT: Carved by Nathan P. Jackson (Tlingit)
and Stephen P. Jackson (Tlingit); painted by
Dorica R. Jackson. Kaats (detail), 2004.
Red cedar, paints. Commissioned by the
museum in 2004.

FREER GALLERY OF ART

The Freer Gallery of Art and the adjacent Arthur M. Sackler Gallery form the Smithsonian's National Museum of Asian Art. The Freer Gallery houses one of the world's finest collections of Asian art, with magnificent holdings that span Neolithic times to the early 20th century. The Italian Renaissance–style building by architect Charles Adams Platt also displays works by American artists from the 19th and early 20th centuries. Among the Freer's many exceptional works is James McNeill Whistler's sumptuously painted Peacock Room, which is permanently on view.

OPPOSITE: James McNeill Whistler (1834–1903). *Harmony in Blue and Gold: The Peacock Room*, 1877. Oil paint and gold leaf on canvas, leather, and wood. Gift of Charles Lang Freer, Freer Gallery of Art. F1904.61.

Independence Avenue (accessible entrance) at 12th Street SW

Mall entrance: Jefferson Drive at 12th Street SW

Open daily from 10 a.m. to 5:30 p.m. Closed December 25

Metrorail: Smithsonian station

Smithsonian information: 202-633-1000

asia.si.edu

In 1923 the Freer Gallery of Art opened to the public as the first fine arts museum on the National Mall and one of the first museums in the United States devoted to Asian art. Detroit industrialist Charles Lang Freer (1854–1919) offered his vast collection of Asian and American art to the nation in 1906. His original gift of nearly 10,000 objects included exceptional art from China, Japan, Korea, South and Southeast Asia, ancient Egypt, and the Islamic world. Freer's gift also featured a significant collection of American art largely dating to the late 19th century as well as the world's largest holdings of diverse works by James McNeill Whistler, including the famed Peacock Room. Paintings by Thomas Wilmer Dewing, Abbott Handerson Thayer, Dwight William Tryon, John Singer Sargent, and other American artists of the late 19th and early 20th century are also part of the permanent collection.

Freer offered his collection to the Smithsonian Institution and, after it was accepted in 1906, he continued to add to his collection. He worked with architect Charles Adams Platt to design the Italianate structure that would house his gift to the nation.

The Freer Gallery of Art preserves and conveys the vision of its founder in presenting Asian and American art. The Gallery's celebrated collection, which has grown through gifts and purchases over the past century, now boasts nearly 26,000 works of art.

Freer began collecting American art in the 1880s. He limited his acquisitions to the work of a few living artists and concentrated especially on Whistler. In 1887 he turned his focus to Asian art, and by the time of his death in 1919 he had assembled an unparalleled collection of Asian masterpieces. Freer once wrote that he attempted to "gather together objects of art covering various periods of production, all of which are harmonious and allied in many ways."

OPPOSITE: James McNeill Whistler (1834–1903). *Variations in Flesh Colour and Green—The Balcony*, 1864–1870; additions 1870–1879. Oil on wood panel. Gift of Charles Lang Freer, Freer Gallery of Art. F1892.23.

LEFT: Katsushika Hokusai (1760–1849). Folio from *Odori hitorigeiko*, Japan. Edo period, 1815 (Bunka 12). Woodblock printed; ink on paper. Purchase, The Gerhard Pulverer Collection—Charles Lang Freer Endowment, Friends of the Freer and Sackler Galleries and the Harold P. Stern Memorial Fund in appreciation of Jeffrey P. Cunard and his exemplary service to the Galleries as chair of the Board of Trustees. FSC-GR-780.222.

BELOW: Zhao Mengfu (1254–1322). Detail, *Sheep and Goat*. China, Yuan dynasty, ca. 1300. Handscroll, ink on paper. Purchase—Charles Lang Freer Endowment, Freer Gallery of Art. F1931.4.

BOTTOM: The Enlightenment, one of four scenes from the life of the Buddha. Pakistan or Afghanistan, Gandhara, Kushan dynasty, late 2nd–early 3rd century. Schist. purchased by Charles Lang Freer Endowment, Freer Gallery of Art. F1949.9.

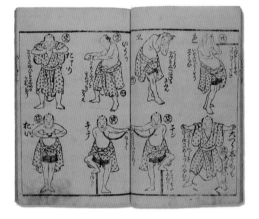

The loggias that surround the Freer's tranquil courtyard and fountain welcome visitors to relax and enjoy the beautiful works of art on view. Today, the building is on the National Register of Historic Places and is a favored destination for those seeking an inspiring and peaceful escape from the bustle of the National Mall.

Works from the Freer Gallery's permanent collection are frequently put on display in an ongoing program of thematic exhibitions. Japanese ceramics, screens, and hanging scrolls; ancient Chinese jades and bronzes; Buddhist art; South Asian sculpture; and arts of the Islamic world are featured in the skylighted galleries. The museum also offers guided tours daily and presents a variety of public concerts, films, and family programs. Learn more at asia.si.edu.

TOP: Tigers, possibly base supports for a bell stand. China, Shaanxi province, Baoji, Middle Western Zhou dynasty. ca. 950–850 BCE. Bronze. Purchase—Charles Lang Freer Endowment, Freer Gallery of Art. F1935.21–.22.

LEFT: *Prince Amar Singh walking in the rain.* India, Mewar, Sisodia dynasty. Reign of Amar Singh II, ca. 1690. Opaque watercolor on paper. Purchase and partial gift made in 2012 from the Catherine and Ralph Benkaim Collection—Charles Lang Freer Endowment, Freer Gallery of Art. F2012.4.3.

OPPOSITE: Charles Lang Freer envisioned the museum's inner courtyard as a quiet place to contemplate art.

GENERAL INFORMATION

ENTRANCES
The main visitors' entrances are located on Jefferson Drive (National Mall side) and on Independence Avenue. A street-level accessible entrance on Independence Avenue has elevator service to the galleries. The Freer connects to the Arthur M. Sackler Gallery through an underground gallery.

INFORMATION DESK
Volunteers staff the information desk located in the lobby near the National Mall entrance from 10 a.m. to 5 p.m. daily.

TOURS
Free guided tours are offered daily, except Wednesdays and federal holidays. Group tours are available with four weeks' advance registration. For more information, go to asia. si.edu/visit; to schedule a group tour, email asiatours@si.edu.

LIBRARY
A Smithsonian library serving the Freer and Sackler is located in the Sackler Gallery. With more than 86,000 volumes, the library is one of the finest repositories of Asian art resources in the United States. Library hours are 10 a.m. to 5 p.m., Monday through Friday, except federal holidays. Visit asia.si.edu/research/library for more information or to search the online catalog.

ARCHIVES
The Archives house more than 160 collections—in excess of 1,000 linear feet of materials—that include personal and professional papers, photography of Asia and the Middle East, graphics, audio tapes, and other forms of documentation related to the museum's collections. Located in the Sackler Gallery, the Archives are open to researchers by appointment; call 202-633-0533. Visit asia.si.edu/research/archives for more information.

BROWSE OUR COLLECTIONS ONLINE
The full and incredibly rich collections of the Freer and Sackler Galleries—more than 44,000 objects—are available online at open.asia.si.edu to search, download, and discover.

FILMS AND PERFORMANCES
The Freer's Meyer Auditorium hosts free concerts and films year-round, presenting both new works and beloved classics. For a full schedule, visit asia.si.edu/events.

ARTHUR M. SACKLER GALLERY

The Arthur M. Sackler Gallery and the Freer Gallery of Art form the Smithsonian's National Museum of Asian Art. The Sackler Gallery, opened on the National Mall in 1987. In addition to beautiful displays from its permanent collection, the Sackler Gallery features national and international exhibitions of exceptional art from Japan, China, South and Southeast Asia, and the Islamic world, ranging from the ancient to the contemporary.

OPPOSITE: The Tibetan Buddhist Shrine Room from the Alice S. Kandell Collection contains objects from Tibet, China, and Mongolia.

1050 Independence Avenue SW

Enter from Enid A. Haupt Garden through ground-level pavilion

Open daily from 10 a.m. to 5:30 p.m. Closed December 25

Metrorail: Smithsonian station

Smithsonian information: 202-633-1000

asia.si.edu

The remarkable collection of Asian art donated by Dr. Arthur M. Sackler (1913–1987) includes ancient Iranian metalwork, Chinese jades and bronzes, and other important works now in the permanent collection. Celebrated Persian and Indian manuscripts and paintings amassed by the French jeweler Henri Vever (1854–1942) were also acquired for the inauguration of the Sackler Gallery. Today the museum houses one of the world's largest holdings of Japanese prints as well as a choice collection of South and Southeast Asian sculpture and a growing number of contemporary Asian photographs. The collection has grown from the initial gift of a thousand objects to nearly 18,000 works of Asian art acquired through gifts and purchases. Additionally, the museum is the site of dynamic public programs and popular events for all visitors.

At the Arthur M. Sackler Gallery, Asia's distinctive artistic and cultural traditions are celebrated through national and international exhibitions of art from other collections and museums. Recent exhibitions have highlighted contemporary Asian photography, Buddhist sculpture from India to China, and a selection of magnificent objects worn and used by empresses during the Qing dynasty.

The Sackler Gallery possesses a large and impressive collection of Japanese prints, dating from the 19th century to the present, as well as illustrated and illuminated manuscripts from Iran and India and one of the finest collections of Central Asian ikats.

Families can learn about Asia through the Sackler's popular ImaginAsia programs, and all visitors enjoy the museum-wide celebrations of

OPPOSITE: *Prophet Muhammad's night journey (Mi'raj)*. Folio from a *Falnama (Book of Omens)*. Iran, Qazvin, Safavid period, mid 1550s–early 1560s. Opaque watercolor, ink, and gold on paper. Purchase—Smithsonian Unrestricted Trust Funds, Smithsonian Collections Acquisition Program, and Dr. Arthur M. Sackler, Arthur M. Sackler Gallery. S1986.253.

BELOW LEFT: Kawase Hasui (1883–1957). *Kiyosu Bridge*. Japan, Showa era, 1931. Woodblock print; ink and color on paper. Robert O. Muller Collection, Arthur M. Sackler Gallery. S2003.8.761.

BELOW: Prajnaparamita Cambodia, Angkor period, ca. 1200. Copper alloy. Gift of Ann and Gilbert Kinney, Arthur M. Sackler Gallery. S2015.26.

the Lunar New Year, Nowruz (in association with the Persian New Year), and the National Cherry Blossom Festival. Visit asia.si.edu/events for more information and up-to-date schedules of activities throughout the museum.

ABOVE: Drinking horn (*rhyton*). Iran or Afghanistan, Sasanian period, fourth century CE. Silver and gilt. Gift of Arthur M. Sackler, Arthur M. Sackler Gallery. S1987.33.

LEFT: *Head of a woman* ("*Miriam*"). Yemen, Kingdom of Qataban, Timna, 1st century BCE–first half of 1st century CE. Alabaster, plaster, lapis lazuli or glass. Gift of the American Foundation for the Study of Man (Wendell and Merilyn Phillips Collection). Sackler Gallery of Art. S2013.2.139.

OPPOSITE: Toyohara Kunichika (1835–1900). *Onoe Kikugorô as Tenjiku Tokubee*. Japan, Meiji era, 1891. Woodblock print; ink and color on paper. Robert O. Muller Collection, Arthur M. Sackler Gallery. S2003.8.2741.

GENERAL INFORMATION

ENTRANCE
Enter from Independence Avenue through a ground-level pavilion and proceed to exhibition areas on three lower levels. The Freer Gallery of Art, with related exhibitions and programs, is accessible by an underground gallery.

INFORMATION DESK
Located in the entrance pavilion, information desks are staffed by volunteers from 10 a.m. to 5 p.m. daily.

TOURS
Free guided tours are offered daily, except Wednesdays and federal holidays. Group tours are available with four weeks' advance registration. For more information, visit asia. si.edu/tour; to schedule a tour, e-mail asiatours@si.edu.

GALLERY SHOP
The shop, located on the first level, features a carefully curated selection of gifts and keepsakes inspired by the museum's collections and Asian cultures. Items include porcelain, crafts, jewelry, textiles, books, prints, and cards.

LIBRARY
A Smithsonian Library serving the Freer and Sackler Galleries is located in the Sackler. The most comprehensive Asian art resource in the United States, the library contains more than 80,000 volumes and regular periodicals. Library hours are 10 a.m. to 5 p.m., Monday through Friday, except federal holidays. Visit asia.si.edu/research/library for more information or to search the online catalog.

ARCHIVES
Researchers may examine the more than 100,000 historical documents and photographic images in the archives, located in the Sackler. The Archives is open by appointment; visit asia.si.edu/research/archives for more information or to request an appointment.

NATIONAL MUSEUM OF AFRICAN ART

Home to the nation's collection of African art, the National Museum of African Art celebrates the rich visual traditions and the diverse cultures of Africa and its diasporas across time, geography, and media. It fosters an appreciation of Africa's arts and civilizations through collections, exhibitions, research, and public programs.

The museum, located on the National Mall, houses its collections, galleries, education facilities, conservation laboratory, research library, and photographic archives.

OPPOSITE: Victor Ekpuk (b. 1964, Nigeria). *Composition #3* (detail), 2009. Graphite and pastel on paper. Gift of the artist and museum purchase. 2010-8-3.

950 Independence Avenue SW
Enter from Enid A. Haupt Garden through ground-level pavilion

Open daily 10 a.m. to 5:30 p.m.

Eliot Elisofon Photographic Archives (202-633-4690), open Tuesday through Thursday by appointment

Warren M. Robbins Library (202-633-4680), open weekdays by appointment

Closed December 25

Metrorail: Smithsonian station

Smithsonian information: 202-633-4600
africa.si.edu

The National Museum of African Art celebrates Africa's rich visual culture across time and geography without regional, media, or historical favor. Founded in 1964 by Warren M. Robbins (1923–2008) to promote cross-cultural understanding through the arts and social sciences, the museum became part of the Smithsonian Institution in 1979. Through its more than 12,000 works of art, dynamic exhibitions, community outreach, and international collaborations, the museum seeks to broadcast and amplify the reach of Africa's arts and underscore the profound historical and contemporary connections Africa has with the United States and the world.

COLLECTIONS

The National Museum of African Art's exhibitions present the finest examples of art from Africa's visual culture across time and geography, without regional, media, or historical favor.

In 2005, the museum acquired by gift the Walt Disney–Tishman African Art Collection, which contains some of the most iconic works of African art. The museum is committed to the ongoing conservation, research, and display of this world-famous collection. The museum also boasts the largest collection of contemporary African art in the United States and, since 1966,

ABOVE: Bullom or Temne artist (Northern or Southern Province, Sierra Leone). Hunting horn, 1494–1500. Ivory, metal. Gift of Walt Disney World Co., a subsidiary of The Walt Disney Company. 2005-6-9.

RIGHT: Chowke artist (Angola or Democratic Republic of the Congo). *Pwo* (face mask). Early 20th century. Wood, plant fiber, pigment, copper alloy. Museum purchase. 85-15-20.

has been actively acquiring the work of some of the world's best-known artists, including El Anatsui, Sammy Baloji, Ibrahim El Salahi, William Kentridge, Julie Mehretu, Wangechi Mutu, and Lynette Yiadom-Boakye. The museum also commissions artworks, including the first-ever land art exhibition installed on the National Mall.

DISCOVER!

The National Museum of African Art's public programs highlight the visual arts of Africa as a catalyst to interdisciplinary teaching and learning, and they promote a deeper understanding of Africa's rich artistic heritage and cultures. Film screenings, guided tours, music and dance programs, scholarly symposia, workshops, and a family-friendly Discovery Room are among the free offerings to the public. Visit africa.si.edu/events for a complete schedule.

Audiovisual loan programs, the collections database, downloadable lesson plans and curriculum guides, online exhibitions, and video conference distance learning expand the museum's mission beyond its walls and connect visitors with Africa and the world.

ABOVE: Mo Abbara (1935–2016, b. Sudan, Mohammed Ahmed Abdalla). Vase, 1990. Porcelainous stoneware. Purchased with funds provided by the Smithsonian Collections Acquisition Program. 96-15-2.

LEFT: Yinka Shonibare CBE (b. 1962, England). *19th Century Kid (Queen Victoria)*, 1999. Cloth, synthetic fiber, dyes, wood, metal, leather. Purchased with funds given in memory of Philip L. Ravenhill, the Sylvia H. Williams Memorial Fund for Acquisitions, Frieda B. Rosenthal, Barbara Croissant and Mark E. Baker. 2000-6-1.

RESEARCH FACILITIES

The National Museum of African Art is a leading research and reference center for the arts of Africa. The state-of-the-art conservation laboratory houses an X-radiography system with digital imaging and serves as an international authority on conserving African art, often collaborating with other institutions to analyze African art materials and identify treatment protocols. The Eliot Elisofon Photographic Archives (EEPA), with 500,000 prints and transparencies, extensive unedited footage, and documentary films, specializes in the collection and preservation of visual materials on Africa's arts, cultures, and environments. The Warren M. Robbins Library contains more than 50,000 volumes on African art and material culture.

The museum continues to advance the field through a robust fellowship program for academics, artists, and conservators.

ABOVE: Bamum artist (Grassfields region, Cameroon). Male figure, late 19th century. Wood, brass, cloth, glass beads, cowrie shells. Gift of Evelyn A. J. Hall and John A. Friede. 85-8-1.

LEFT: Nontsikelelo "Lolo" Veleko (b. 1977, South Africa). *Kepi in Bree Street*, from the Beauty Is in the Eye of the Beholder series, 2006. Digital print with pigment dyes on cotton paper. Purchased with funds provided by the Annie Laurie Aitken Endowment. 2011-7-1.4.

OPPOSITE: Solomon Osagie Alonge (1911–1994, b. Nigeria). *Oba Akenzua II (Reigned 1933–79) Greets Queen Elizabeth on a Royal Visit, Benin City, Nigeria*, ca. 1956. Hand-colored silver gelatin print. Chief S. O. Alonge Collection. Eliot Elisofon Photographic Archives. EEPA 2009-007-1796.

GENERAL INFORMATION

INFORMATION DESK
In the entrance pavilion

ACCESSIBILITY
The museum public spaces, exhibitions, and programs are accessible to visitors with disabilities. The main entrance, located on Independence Avenue near the gate to the Enid A. Haupt Garden, accommodates visitors in wheelchairs and those with strollers. All levels, exhibition spaces, and public facilities are accessible by elevator.

TOURS
Museum tours are offered for individuals on a walk-in basis at select times. Tours for school and community groups are available by appointment. To request a tour schedule or make an appointment, visit africa.si.edu/education.

SHOPPING
African jewelry, textiles, handicrafts, musical recordings, books, exhibition catalogs, posters, and postcards are for sale.

MEMBERSHIP
Support the National Museum of African Art! Join the community at africa.si.edu/support.

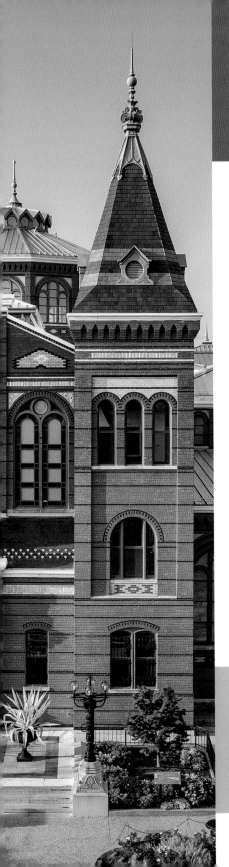

ARTS AND INDUSTRIES BUILDING

The Arts and Industries Building opened in 1881 as the first National Museum of the United States. Standing just east of the Castle, this historic space debuted 140 years ago and introduced millions to a rapidly growing collection of the "wonders of the world." Built with the ticket proceeds from the 1876 Centennial Exposition in Philadelphia, its soaring halls have showcased everything from national treasures like the Star-Spangled Banner to world-changing inventions like Edison's light bulb, the Wright Flyer, and NASA rockets. Much more than a museum, the Arts and Industries Building was a catalyst that drove a young nation forward.

OPPOSITE: The Arts and Industries Building, seen from the National Mall, was the Smithsonian's first purpose-built museum.
CREDIT: Ron Blunt

900 Jefferson Drive SW (next to the Smithsonian Castle). Opening scheduled from June 2021 through mid-2022, then closed for renovation (check aib.si.edu for updates)

Metrorail: Smithsonian station

Smithsonian information: 202-633-1000

aib.si.edu

Over the decades, the building incubated nearly every other Smithsonian museum. The Natural History Museum, American History Museum, Portrait Gallery, American Art Museum, Freer Gallery, and Postal Museum all started here before expanding to their own spaces. The building became a center for experimentation, hosting early chemistry labs, the nation's rare books library, groundbreaking exhibits that incorporated light and sound, and even the Smithsonian's first computer.

The Arts and Industries Building is considered one of the best-preserved examples of 19th-century world exposition architecture in the United States. Designed by Adolf Cluss, it was inspired by World's Fair pavilions and intended to complement the Castle and fulfill "modern demands of perfect safety and elegance of construction." Soaring, light-filled halls, decorative ironwork, and an impressive rotunda provided a perfect backdrop for the many noteworthy exhibits it was intended to display. If built today, it would be considered a "green" sustainable building, with fresh air and natural light in every space and local materials used wherever possible.

Never fully renovated, the building closed completely in 2004 because of structural concerns. A partial renovation in 2014 replaced the roof and nearly a thousand windows and restored the exterior to its 1881 appearance. For the first time in 140 years, we have an extraordinary opportunity to reimagine the building in its entirety and renew its original purpose: to be an incubator for big ideas and bold discoveries that bring people together.

The Smithsonian is currently reenergizing the Arts and Industries Building with plans for a long-term renovation and reopening. Since 2016 the building has become a new home for forward-thinking special events and pop-up exhibitions and performances on the National Mall. In 2021 and 2022, the Arts and Industries Building will stage FUTURES, a dynamic, multidisciplinary festival that will invite visitors to imagine not just one future, but many possible futures that we can shape together. With an array of ideas, innovations, and solutions designed to create a toolkit for the future, FUTURES will invite all Americans—in person, online, and in their own communities—to ask bold questions and think more hopefully about what is to come.

LEFT: Large rockets flanked the north entrance of the Smithsonian Arts and Industries Building during the 1950s to 1970s in an exhibit called "Rocket Row."

OPPOSITE: The Arts and Industries Building, closed since 2004, will reopen to the public in 2021 and 2022 before closing again for further renovation. CREDIT: Farrah Skeiky.

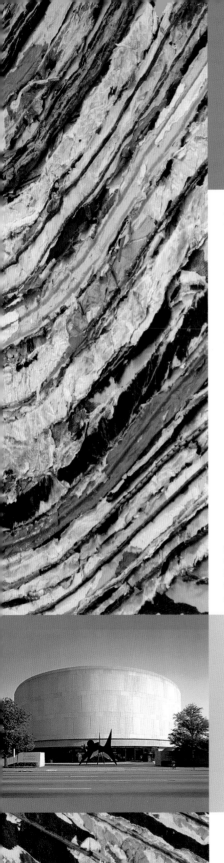

HIRSHHORN MUSEUM AND SCULPTURE GARDEN

As the Smithsonian's showcase for modern and contemporary art, the Hirshhorn Museum and Sculpture Garden provides a comprehensive look at art from the first stirrings of modernism in the 19th century to the most recent developments in the art world. Sculpture by modern masters (much of it situated outdoors), international modernist works of the postwar era, and contemporary art are particular attractions. American and European Cubism, Social Realism, Surrealism, Geometric Abstraction, and Expressionism trace modern art past the mid–20th century.

OPPOSITE: Mark Bradford (b. 1961). *Pickett's Charge*, 2017, as installed at the Hirshhorn. Mixed media on canvas. Collection of the artist. Courtesy Hauser & Wirth. Photo: Joshua White.

Independence Avenue at Seventh Street SW

Building and Plaza entered from Independence Avenue; Plaza and Sculpture Garden entered from National Mall

Open daily. Building, 10 a.m. to 5:30 p.m.; Plaza, 7:30 a.m. to 5:30 p.m.; Sculpture Garden, 7:30 a.m. to dusk. Closed December 25

Metrorail: L'Enfant Plaza station

Smithsonian information: 202-633-1000

hirshhorn.si.edu

This striking museum of modern and contemporary art is named after the dedicated and enthusiastic American art collector Joseph H. Hirshhorn (1899–1981). His gifts and bequest to the nation of more than 12,000 works are the nucleus of a dynamic collection that remains current through purchases and gifts from many donors. When the museum opened in 1974, the Smithsonian offered, for the first time, a history of modern art in a building and sunken garden that were bold, even daring, by contemporary architectural standards. Today the museum is, for many visitors, the most challenging and visually stimulating of the Smithsonian's attractions on the National Mall. Museumgoers may be dazzled or intrigued by the works on view—the experience is seldom boring. Art, especially new art, can evoke powerful responses.

A PLACE FOR SCULPTURE

Sculpture was a special passion of the museum's founding donor, and the Hirshhorn's sculpture collection is one of the most distinguished in the world. Sculptures by international artists can be seen throughout the museum as well as on the outdoor fountain plaza and amid the greenery along pathways in the garden. There, adjacent to the National Mall, are several signature works, including Auguste Rodin's figure ensemble *The Burghers of Calais* (1884–1889); compositions by midcentury sculptural giants Henry Moore and Beverly Pepper; and Mark di Suvero's definitive, soaring red-steel construction *Are Years What? (for Marianne Moore)* (1967), to name a few.

ABOVE: Constantin Brancusi (1876–1957). *Torso of a Young Man*, 1924. Bronze on stone and wood bases. Gift of Joseph H. Hirshhorn, 1966 (66.661). © Constantin Brancusi/ARS, NY.

BELOW LEFT: Beverly Pepper (1922–2020). *Ex Cathedra*, 1967. Stainless steel and paint. Gift of Joseph H. Hirshhorn, 1980 (80.37).

BELOW RIGHT: Mark di Suvero (b. 1933). *Are Years What? (for Marianne Moore)*, 1967. Steel and paint. Joseph H. Hirshhorn Purchase Fund and Gift of the Institute of Scrap Recycling Industries, by exchange, 1999 (99.19). © Mark di Suvero/Spacetime C. C.

. . . AND THE ART OF OUR TIME

Joseph Hirshhorn was dedicated to the art and artists of his own era, and because he tended to purchase many pieces by artists he particularly admired, the museum is able to present in-depth explorations of such groundbreaking figures as Alexander Calder, Barbara Hepworth, Willem de Kooning, and Clyfford Still.

Continuing that tradition, the museum remains committed to acquiring and exhibiting work by both emerging and established contemporary international artists. Recent acquisition galleries feature the latest pieces to enter the collection and have included such visitor favorites as Alicja Kwade's visually disorienting mirrored installation *WeltenLinie* (2018) and Huang Yong Ping's ambitious live-plant and tile installation *Abbottabad* (2013). The inner-ring galleries on the museum's second

ABOVE: Doug Aitken (b. 1968). *SONG 1*, 2012. Video projection on exterior of the Hirshhorn. Joseph H. Hirshhorn Bequest Fund and Anonymous Gift, 2012, dedicated in honor of Kerry Brougher's service to the Hirshhorn Museum and Sculpture Garden (2000–2014) (12.9).

BELOW: Barbara Kruger (b. 1945). *Belief+Doubt*, 2012. Installation in lower-level lobby. © Barbara Kruger. Photo by Cathy Carver.

and third floors serve as dynamic spaces for site-specific projects, such as Linn Meyers's 400-foot-long wall drawing *Our View from Here* (exhibited May 2016–August 2017) and Mark Bradford's monumental eight-painting cycle *Pickett's Charge* (on view through 2021). Similarly, Barbara Kruger designed her text-based work *Belief+Doubt* (2012) as an installation for the museum's shop and lower-level lobby. The Hirshhorn will continue to engage contemporary artists to create spaces that push boundaries and offer visitors experiences that inspire.

The museum, which often screens works by artists and filmmakers from around the world, also highlights the growing importance of new media, and thus moving-image exhibitions and film series have long been key parts of the Hirshhorn's program. In 2012, the museum collaborated with Doug Aitken to present his 360-degree projection *SONG 1* on the building's façade. Aitken created the colorful moving-image piece with the Hirshhorn's unique architecture in mind. More recently, performance

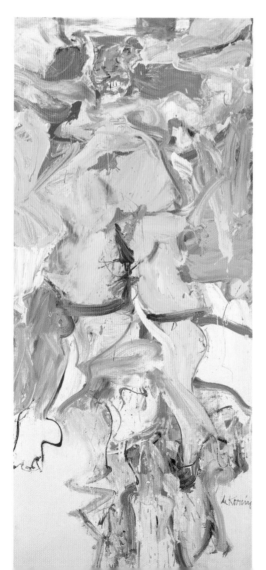

LEFT: Willem de Kooning (1904–1997). *Woman, Sag Harbor* (detail), 1964. Oil and charcoal on wood. Gift of Joseph H. Hirshhorn, 1966 (66.1209). © The Willem de Kooning Foundation / ARS, NY.

OPPOSITE: Georgia O'Keeffe (1887–1986). *Goat's Horn with Red*, 1945. Pastel on paperboard, mounted on paperboard. Gift of Joseph H. Hirshhorn, 1972 (72.217). © Georgia O'Keeffe / ARS, NY.

has become a staple of programming at the museum. Ragnar Kjartansson's eponymous exhibition (October 2016–January 2017) marked the first time that a live performance was on view for the duration of an exhibition, and in 2018, the museum added its first performative artwork to the collection with the acquisition of Tino Sehgal's *This You* (2006).

Rotating collection exhibitions on all levels of the museum demonstrate the diversity of styles, subjects, and media pursued by an international mix of artists. They have focused on such concepts as absence as a means of expression, the reexamination of popular modes of address, and the renewed interest in sublime encounters with art. Important monographic and thematic special exhibitions fill the second-level galleries in a dynamic array of presentations that offer fresh contexts in which to explore modern and contemporary art and new ways to look at the museum's diverse holdings. The galleries on each level continually present a blend of familiar masterpieces and innovative recent works that are sure to intrigue and engage newcomers as well as frequent visitors to the Hirshhorn.

LOOK, LEARN, CREATE

The Hirshhorn offers a range of educational experiences for young and old alike, including lectures and tours by artists and curators, independent film series, informative tours of the permanent collection, and an array of programs, workshops, and activities. Serving visitors with all levels of interest in modern and contemporary art through conversation and dialogue-based tours, Gallery Guides work to engage visitors in open discussions about art, and a rotating schedule of free special tours,

sketching and writing sessions, talks, and one-on-ones with visiting and local artists is offered.

The popular Meet the Artist series, begun in 2000, brings notable artists from around the world to Washington for lectures and discussions about their creative process and recent work. Speakers have included such influential figures as Robert Irwin, Pat Steir, Carolee Schneemann, Ai Weiwei, Anish Kapoor, Marilyn Minter, and Laure Prouvost.

ARTLAB, the Hirshhorn's digital art studio for teens 13 to 19, provides free access to the latest tech, a wide range of art materials, and one-on-one mentorship from professional artists. Students can take part in weekly open studios, join a production team, learn about upcoming internship opportunities, or apply to become an emerging artist. Younger children can attend twice-weekly Storytimes, which pair read-aloud tales with art, and monthly Maker Mornings, which offer hands-on, kid-appropriate interactive projects.

OPPOSITE TOP: Jeff Wall (b. 1946). *A Villager from Aricakoyu Arriving in Mahmutbey-Istanbul, September 1997*, 1997. Cibachrome transparency, aluminum light box, and fluorescent lamps. Joseph H. Hirshhorn Bequest Fund, 1998 (98.9). © Jeff Wall.

OPPOSITE MIDDLE: Dana Hoey (b. 1966). *Waimea*, 2000. C-print on Fujiflex mounted on plastic panel. Gift of Heather and Tony Podesta Collection, Falls Church, VA, 2001 (0.15). © Dana Hoey / Petzel, NY.

OPPOSITE BOTTOM: Ai Weiwei (b. 1957). *Cube Light*, 2008. Stainless steel, glass, electrical wiring, and lightbulbs. Joseph H. Hirshhorn Bequest and Purchase Funds, 2012 (12.12). © Ai Weiwei.

A BOLD SETTING

Gordon Bunshaft (1909–1990), winner in 1988 of the Pritzker Prize in architecture, designed the Hirshhorn. Redesigns of the Sculpture Garden in 1981 and the plaza in 1993 increased accessibility and enhanced the placement of sculpture with additional greenery. The dynamic and unorthodox building—82 feet high and 231 feet in diameter—encircles an open courtyard and an asymmetrically placed bronze fountain. The exterior wall is a solid surface broken by only one 70-foot-long window in the third-level Abram Lerner Room, from which visitors can enjoy a spectacular view of the National Mall. Floor-to-ceiling windows define the inner core, which overlooks the fountain. Four massive piers elevate the concrete structure above the walled plaza.

In the lobby, Dolcezza Café offers coffee and pastries, as well as gelato in warmer seasons. The recessed Sculpture Garden across Jefferson Drive, with its rectangular reflecting pool, provides a peaceful area for viewing art. Outdoors at the Hirshhorn, benches, shaded areas, and fountainside tables provide attractive spots in which to linger.

HIRSHHORN EYE

Want to get up close with the Hirshhorn's art and artists? Meet Hirshhorn Eye (HI), our innovative instant mobile art guide that lets you scan artworks, learn more about the fascinating artists and stories behind the works on view, and watch exclusive videos on your smartphone. To get started, just visit hi.si.edu on your device's web browser.

LEFT: Robert Gober (b. 1954). *Untitled*, 1990. Wax, cotton, wood, leather shoe, and human hair. Joseph H. Hirshhorn Purchase Fund, 1990 (90.15). © Robert Gober / Matthew Marks Gallery, NY.

BELOW: Andy Warhol (1928–1987). *Self-Portrait*, 1986. Synthetic polymer and silkscreen ink on linen. Partial Gift of the Andy Warhol Foundation for the Visual Arts and Partial Purchase, Smithsonian Collections Acquisition Program and Joseph H. Hirshhorn Bequest Fund, 1995 (95.1). © The Andy Warhol Foundation for the Visual Arts / ARS, NY.

GENERAL INFORMATION

INFORMATION DESK
The desk, located in the lobby and staffed from 10 a.m. to 4 p.m. daily, offers information about exhibitions and events.

GUIDES
Gallery Guides are available to answer questions and spark discussion in the galleries between 10:30 a.m. and 4:30 p.m. Wednesday through Sunday. The Guides also give tours at 12:30 p.m. most days. Ask for details at the information desk. Tours for groups with up to 60 participants can be scheduled with four weeks' advance notice. Tours of the Sculpture Garden are available June through October and at other times upon request, weather permitting. The Programs Department offers tours in French, Spanish, and German upon request; for further information, call 202-633-EDUC (3382).

ACCESSIBILITY
The museum provides American Sign Language (ASL) tours and visual description tours for visitors and their companions. Please check the Hirshhorn website for an upcoming tour. Visitors can also navigate the Hirshhorn using Aira, a free app that connects visitors with sighted agents who provide on-demand visual descriptions. This subscription service is free to Smithsonian visitors who are connected to the internet.

PUBLIC PROGRAMS
Free films, lectures, symposia, and talks by artists are presented regularly in the Marion and Gustave Ring Auditorium on the lower level. Other programs include gallery talks, workshops for a variety of audiences, family art activities, summer music concerts, and programs for teachers, schools, and community groups. For information, call 202-633-EDUC (3382) or visit hirshhorn.si.edu.

SHOPPING
The museum store offers exhibition catalogs, postcards, books on art, and gifts and jewelry related to the museum's programs.

ABOVE: Martial Raysse (b. 1936). *Made in Japan*, 1964. Photomechanical reproductions and wallpaper with airbrush ink, gouache, ink, tacks, peacock feathers, and plastic flies on paper mounted on fiberboard. Gift of Joseph H. Hirshhorn, 1972 (72.242). © 2015 Martial Raysse / ARS, NY / ADAGP, Paris.

NATIONAL POSTAL MUSEUM

The National Postal Museum is a family-friendly museum that explores the history of the nation's postal service and the beauty and meaning of the world's postage stamps. Visitors can enjoy more than thirty audiovisual and interactive areas, travel on the first American postal road, sit in a stagecoach and a semi-truck cab, and create a stamp collection to bring home with them. Exhibitions focus on worldwide postage stamps, transportation, letters, and more.

OPPOSITE: The museum atrium has a 90-foot-high ceiling with three vintage airmail planes suspended overhead, a reconstructed railway mail car, an 1851 stagecoach, a 1931 Ford Model A postal truck, and a contemporary Long Life Vehicle postal truck.

2 Massachusetts Avenue at First Street NE (in the old Washington City Post Office Building next to Union Station)

Open daily from 10 a.m. to 5:30 p.m. Closed December 25

Metrorail: Union Station

Museum information: 202-633-5550

postalmuseum.si.edu

Mail touches everyone, making the boundaries of postal history limitless. America's postal history can be explored through objects as small as stamps and as large as airplanes. It is expressed in heartrending letters from soldiers on foreign battlefields and through the explosion of direct-mail marketing. America's postal service was the force behind the creation of commercial aviation. It helped push the development of cross-country stagecoach routes and railroads. It ensured the development and perpetual maintenance of rural roads. Thousands of African Americans were first able to obtain government employment in the postal service. America's postal history is the story of the people who made the service work and those

ABOVE: This badge was worn by a pilot in the Post Office Department's Aerial Mail Service, which operated from 1918 to 1927. More than 32 postal pilots died pioneering new air routes during that period.

who used it. It is the history of mail and the American people.

The National Postal Museum opened on July 30, 1993. Located on Capitol Hill, the museum is housed in the former City Post Office Building, a classic Beaux Arts–style structure designed by Daniel Burnham and built between 1911 and 1914. (The ornate historic lobby that today is the museum's foyer once served as the main customer service area.) The museum has 35,000 square feet of exhibition space, a research library, a stamp store, and a museum store.

OPPOSITE: Learn how to spot telltale signs of mail fraud and uncover how the US Postal Inspection Service has solved some of the nation's most notorious crimes.

TOP: Public school students from Washington, DC, learn how to mail letters at the National Postal Museum.

ABOVE: The lone post rider and horse, pictured in this 1869 stamp proof, were the backbone of the American postal system for more than two centuries.

BINDING THE NATION

This gallery traces events from colonial times through the 19th century, stressing the importance of written communication in the development of the new nation. As early as 1673, regular mail was carried between New York and Boston following Indian trails. As co-deputy postmaster for the colonies, Benjamin Franklin played a key role in establishing mail service. After the Revolution, Americans recognized that the postal service, and the news and information it carried, was essential to binding the nation together. By 1800, mail was carried over more than 9,000 miles of postal roads. On the eve of the Civil War, the Butterfield Overland Mail stagecoach line and the famed Pony Express connected the east and west coasts by land for the first time.

CUSTOMERS AND COMMUNITIES

By the turn of the 20th century, the nation's population was expanding, as was mail volume and the need for personal mail delivery. Crowded cities and the requirements of rural Americans inspired the invention of new delivery methods. Facets of the developing system and its important role in the fabric of the nation are explored through photographs, mail vehicles, a variety of rural mailboxes, and other artifacts.

Parcel Post Service helped usher in an era of consumerism by the early 20th century that foreshadowed massive mechanization, automation, and the mail-order industry. Today, mail service is a vital conduit for business.

MOVING THE MAIL

The postal service was constantly on the lookout for the fastest transportation system available, from post riders to stagecoaches, automobiles, and trucks, to trains and airplanes. After the Civil War, postal officials placed railway mail clerks aboard trains to sort the mail while it was carried between towns and cities across the country. In 1918, airmail service was established on a regular basis between New York,

Philadelphia, and Washington, DC. Airmail contracts provided funding for the development of the commercial aviation industry.

Visitors will discover the story of Owney, a dog who became the mascot of the Railway Mail Service and traveled thousands of miles by train across the United States.

MAIL CALL

Personal letters are vivid windows into history. Rotating exhibits in this gallery convey the stories of families and friends who are bound together by letters over distance and across time. The highlight of Mail Call is a poignant video that explores how mail sustains the bond between military service members and their loved ones back home.

TOP: This handstamp was salvaged from USS *Oklahoma*, which sank at Pearl Harbor in 1941.

ABOVE: The Inverted Jenny, issued for the first scheduled US airmail flight in 1918, is the world's most famous stamp error.

LEFT: Concord coaches, such as this Downing & Son coach from 1851, could hold up to 12 passengers and the mail.

WILLIAM H. GROSS STAMP GALLERY

Amazing stories unfold from the National Postal Museum's world-renowned stamp collections in the William H. Gross Stamp Gallery. Stamps from the United States and around the world are on display in the museum's state-of-the-art gallery, which offers visitors permanent access to spectacular rarities such as the first US postage stamps issued in 1847; mail that survived the *Titanic* and *Hindenburg* disasters; the 24-cent inverted Jenny airmail stamp of 1918; and stamp designs sketched by President Franklin D. Roosevelt.

Since Great Britain issued the first adhesive postage stamp in 1840, these little pieces of paper have provided gateways to history, geography, biography, science, music, art, and more. Stamps record the histories and cultures of all nations, connecting people and places worldwide. They show how people from different cultures have depicted themselves and others over time and reflect innovations in design, printing, and transportation. The Gross Stamp Gallery contains examples from every country in the world that has ever produced stamps, including many countries that no longer exist.

ABOVE: The William H. Gross Stamp Gallery features a world-class stamp collection, with beautiful stamp art on display.

LEFT AND BELOW: Dozens of original US stamp illustrations, such as this 1980 portrait of surveyor and scientist Benjamin Banneker, are displayed in the National Stamp Salon, and some are on loan from the United States Postal Service.

GENERAL INFORMATION

ENTRANCE
On First St. NE near the corner of Massachusetts Ave. The William H. Gross Stamp Gallery is on the lobby level. There are elevators or escalators down to the Atrium level.

TOURS
Scheduled tours for students and groups of ten or more are available. Reservations for these tours must be made three weeks in advance. For a walk-in tour schedule, or to make reservations for a student or group tour, visit the museum's website.

ACCESSIBILITY
The museum has two accessible entrances with ramps: First Street and North Capitol Street via US Post Office (when the museum elevator is out of service, this is the only accessible entrance to the museum). Visual description tours are available for visitors with visual impairments. One week's advance notice is recommended, but not required.

PUBLIC PROGRAMS
An array of public programs offers visitors fresh perspectives on mail in their lives. Museum programs include hands-on workshops, interactive family programs, films, lectures, performances, and much more. Sign language and oral interpreters for programs and tours require two weeks' advance notice. For more information about upcoming public programs, visit the museum's website.

RESEARCH FACILITIES
With more than 40,000 volumes and manuscripts, the museum's library is among the world's largest facilities for postal history and philatelic research. The library features a specimen study room, an audiovisual viewing room, and a rare book collection. Open by appointment, Monday through Friday, from 10 a.m. to 4 p.m.; call 202-633-5543 to schedule a visit.

SHOPPING
Located near the escalators at the museum entrance, the museum store offers posters, T-shirts, stationery, postcards, pins, first-day covers, stamp-collector kits, stamp- and postal-related souvenirs, books for all ages on postal-history subjects and letter collections, and a selection of philatelic publications.

STAMP STORE
Operated by the US Postal Service, the stamp store is located opposite the museum store. Visitors may purchase a variety of current stamps and other commemorative stamp items.

US POST OFFICE
Accessible from the lower level of the museum.

INFORMATION DESK
Off the lobby

ABOVE: The Post Office Department promoted its speedy new service with posters in post offices across the country.

ABOVE: Roger Shimomura (b. 1939). *Shimomura Crossing the Delaware*, 2010. Acrylic on canvas. Acquired through the generosity of Raymond L. Ocampo Jr., Sandra Oleksy Ocampo, and Robert P. Ocampo. © 2010, Roger Shimomura.

RIGHT: Marshall D. Rumbaugh (born 1948). *Rosa Parks*, 1983. Limewood and paint.

NATIONAL PORTRAIT GALLERY

The National Portrait Gallery tells the story of the United States through the people who have shaped its history and culture. Known for its remarkable collection of presidential portraits, including Gilbert Stuart's "Lansdowne" painting of George Washington, the museum also presents special exhibitions that highlight some of the nation's most influential individuals— past and present.

Eighth and F Streets NW

Open daily from 11:30 a.m. to 7 p.m.
Closed December 25

Metrorail: Gallery Place/Chinatown station

Museum information: 202-633-8300

Smithsonian information: 202-633-1000

npg.si.edu

Generations of remarkable Americans are kept in the company of their fellow citizens at the National Portrait Gallery. The museum presents the wonderful diversity of individuals who have left and who are still leaving their marks on our country and our culture. Through the visual and performing arts, we feature leaders such as George Washington and Martin Luther King Jr., artists such as Mary Cassatt and George Gershwin, activists such as Sequoyah and Rosa Parks, and icons of pop culture such as Babe Ruth and Marilyn Monroe, among thousands of others. They all link us to our past, our present, and our future. For anyone fascinated by famous Americans and their stories, the National Portrait Gallery is a must-visit destination.

The Portrait Gallery reopened in 2006 after an extensive six-year renovation of its National Historic Landmark building. The structure itself, begun in 1836 for the US Patent Office, stood for the highest aspirations of the nation. Praised by Walt Whitman as "the noblest of Washington buildings," it was saved from the wrecking ball

ABOVE: Betsy Graves Reyneau (1888–1964). *George Washington Carver*, 1942. Oil on canvas. Gift of the George Washington Carver Memorial Committee. © Peter Edward Fayard.

OPPOSITE: Gilbert Stuart (1755–1828). *George Washington* ("Lansdowne" Portrait), 1796. Oil on canvas. Acquired as a gift to the nation through the generosity of the Donald W. Reynolds Foundation.

in 1958 and then welcomed the opening of the National Portrait Gallery in 1968. That was no accident. Pierre L'Enfant, in his design for the new federal city, had envisioned for this site a place to honor the nation's heroes. In our own time, a building has been reborn and a vision fulfilled.

Portraiture as an art form is alive across the United States. In several exhibitions each year, the National Portrait Gallery showcases new talent and new faces. In Portraiture Now, the museum continues a new series of exhibitions featuring contemporary artists who explore with imagination and skill the age-old art of depicting the figure. Through paintings, sculptures, works on paper, and time-based media, artists bring portraiture into the 21st century.

One of the building's most popular exhibitions is *America's Presidents*, which presents the nation's only complete collection of presidential portraits outside the White House. This installation lies at the heart of

the Portrait Gallery's mission to tell the country's history through the individuals who have shaped it. Visitors can experience an enhanced, extended display of images that shed light on the lives of every former president of the United States. Explore Gilbert Stuart's "Lansdowne" portrait of George Washington, the famous "cracked-plate" photograph of Abraham Lincoln, and renowned likenesses of Lyndon Johnson, Jimmy Carter, Richard Nixon, and George H. W. Bush.

Adjacent to *America's Presidents*, visitors will find *The Struggle for Justice,* which showcases individuals from the museum's permanent collection who have played significant roles in advancing civil rights and justice. The installation includes a range of activists, from Frederick Douglass and Susan B. Anthony to Martin Luther King Jr. and Cesar Chavez, who all struggled on behalf of disenfranchised Americans.

A "Conversation about America" is on view in a series of 17 galleries and alcoves, titled *American Origins,* arranged chronologically. The exhibition highlights such figures as Pocahontas, Alexander Hamilton, Henry Clay, Nathaniel Hawthorne, and Harriet Beecher Stowe.

Three galleries devoted to the Civil War— "Faces of Discord"—examine the conflict in depth. A selection of modern photographic prints produced from Mathew Brady's original

BOTTOM LEFT: Alexander Gardner (1821–1882). *Abraham Lincoln*, 1865. Albumen silver print.

BOTTOM RIGHT: Sallie E. Garrity (ca. 1862–1907). *Ida B. Wells-Barnett*, ca. 1893. Albumen silver print.

OPPOSITE: Unidentified artist, after Simon van de Passe. *Pocahontas*, after 1616. Oil on canvas. Gift of the A. W. Mellon Educational and Charitable Trust.

MISS GARRITY.
PHOTOGRAPHER.
CHICAGO.

negatives complements the exhibition. Selections from the Portrait Gallery's remarkable collection of daguerreotypes (the earliest practical form of photography) make the National Portrait Gallery the first major museum to create a permanent exhibition space for daguerreotype portraits.

Each year, a gallery within the museum called "One Life" sheds light on an individual by exploring his or her legacy in depth.

Four galleries opening onto the museum's magnificent third-floor Great Hall showcase the major cultural, scientific, and political figures of the 20th and 21st centuries. Two exhibitions on the third-floor mezzanines highlight particular themes in American life. *Bravo!* features individuals who have brought the performing arts to life, from the late 19th century through the present. *Champions* salutes the dynamic

Ætatis suæ 21. Aº. 1616.

aloaks als Rebecka daughter to the mighty Prince
owhatan Emperour of Attanoughkomouck als Virginia
onverted and baptized in the Christian faith, and
Wife to the worll Mr Tho: Rolff.

American sports figures whose impact has extended beyond the athletic realm and made them a part of the larger story of the nation.

Every three years, the National Portrait Gallery invites artists from across the nation to participate in its Outwin Boochever Portrait Competition. The triennial competition and resulting exhibition encourage artists living in the United States to submit a recent portrait. The events celebrate excellence and innovation, with a strong focus on the variety of portrait media used by artists today.

The National Portrait Gallery offers a lively selection of public programs that demonstrate the power of portraiture. Visitors learn about people who have significantly influenced American history and culture. The department develops innovative, thoughtful programming for audiences from near and far. Using the exhibitions as a catalyst for these educational offerings, the collections come alive through interactive tours, workshops, and courses. For details on the National Portrait Gallery's free programs, including its digital offerings, check the museum's website.

LEFT: Alexis Rodríguez-Duarte, photographer, and Tico Torres, stylist. *¡Yo soy de Cuba la Voz, Guantanamera!* Inkjet print. 1994 (printed 2016). Acquisition made possible through the Smithsonian Latino Initiatives Pool, administered by the Smithsonian Latino Center. © 1994, Alexis Rodríguez-Duarte.

GENERAL INFORMATION

INFORMATION DESK
Located in the lobby.

TOURS
Walk-in tours with museum docents are offered. For information on group tours, call 202-633-1000.

PUBLIC PROGRAMS
Free public programs include gallery talks, films, illustrated lectures, artist workshops, family days, and performances of music, dance, and theater. For information, call 202-633-1000 or visit npg.si.edu.

SHOPPING
The museum stores, located on the first floor, feature collection-inspired gifts, books, note cards, posters, calendars, jewelry, and more.

DINING
The Courtyard Café offers casual dining with a seasonal menu of American dishes. It is open from 11:30 a.m. to 4 p.m.; coffee, beer and wine, and light fare are available until 6:30 p.m.

INTERNET
Free internet is available throughout the building. Stay connected with the National Portrait Gallery via social media through Facebook, Instagram (@smithsoniannpg), Twitter (@smithsoniannpg), and YouTube (youtube.com/NatlPortraitGallery).

ABOVE: Edward Hopper
(1882–1967). *Cape Cod Morning*
(detail), 1950. Oil on canvas. Gift
of the Sara Roby Foundation.

RIGHT: Hiram Maristany.
Hydrant: In the Air, 1963.
Gelatin silver print. Museum
purchase through the
Smithsonian Latino Initiatives
Pool, administered by the
Smithsonian Latino Center.
© 1963, Hiram Maristany.

SMITHSONIAN AMERICAN ART MUSEUM

The nation's first American art collection comprises more than 400 years of painting, sculpture, time-based media art, photography, graphic art, and folk and self-taught art. The museum's historic Greek Revival building in the heart of the nation's capital has been meticulously renovated with expanded permanent collection galleries and the Luce Foundation Center for American Art, the first visible art storage and study center in Washington, DC. A wide array of free public programs is offered; visit americanart. si.edu for information.

Eighth and F Streets NW

Open daily from 11:30 a.m. to 7 p.m.
Closed December 25

Metrorail: Gallery Place/Chinatown station

Museum information: 202-633-7970

americanart.si.edu

The Smithsonian American Art Museum, the nation's first collection of American art, is an unparalleled record of the American experience. The collection captures the aspirations, character, and imagination of the American people throughout four centuries. The museum is the home to one of the largest and most inclusive collections of American art in the world. Its artworks reveal key aspects of America's rich artistic and cultural history from the colonial period to today.

More than 7,000 artists are represented in the museum's collection, including masters such as John Singleton Copley, Winslow Homer, John Singer Sargent, Mary Cassatt, Georgia O'Keeffe, Edward Hopper, Jacob Lawrence, David Hockney, Lee Friedlander, Nam June Paik, Martin Puryear, and Robert Rauschenberg. Artworks in the collection reveal key aspects of America's rich artistic and cultural history from the colonial period to today.

The museum has been a leader in collecting and exhibiting the finest works of American art. Pioneering collections include time-based media art and video games; photography from its origins in the 19th century to contemporary works; images of western expansion; realist art from the first half of the 20th century; folk and self-taught art; and work by African American and Latino artists. The museum has the country's largest collection of New Deal art and murals and the largest collection of American sculpture.

As a major center for research in American art, the museum includes such resources as the Inventory of American Paintings executed before 1914, with data on nearly 290,000 works; the Peter A. Juley & Sons collection of 127,000 historic photographs; the Pre-1877 Art Exhibition Catalog Index; the Inventory of American Sculpture, with information on more than 85,000 indoor and outdoor works; the Nam June Paik archive; and the Joseph Cornell Study Center.

TOP: Malcah Zeldis (b. 1931). *Miss Liberty Celebration*, 1987. Oil on corrugated cardboard. Gift of Herbert Waide Hemphill Jr. © 1987, Malcah Zeldis.

ABOVE: Robert Reid (1862–1929). *The Mirror*, ca. 1910. Oil on canvas. Gift of William T. Evans.

OPPOSITE: Georgia O'Keeffe (1887–1986). *Manhattan*, 1932. Oil on canvas. Gift of the Georgia O'Keeffe Foundation.

LUCE FOUNDATION CENTER FOR AMERICAN ART

The Luce Foundation Center, the first visible art study and storage center in Washington, provides new ways to experience American art with more than 3,300 artworks from the

museum's collection on display. It features
paintings densely hung on screens; sculptures,
craftworks, and folk art objects arranged on
shelves; and portrait miniatures, bronze medals,
and jewelry in drawers that slide open with the
touch of a button. Interpretive materials and
artist biographies are available for every work.

COLLECTIONS

The Smithsonian American Art Museum's
collection tells the story of America through
the visual arts. Colonial portraiture, 19th-
century landscapes, American Impressionism,
20th-century realism and abstraction, New
Deal projects, sculpture, photography, prints
and drawings, African American art, Latino
art, self-taught and folk art, and time-based
media art are featured in the collection.
Contemporary American crafts are presented
at the Smithsonian American Art Museum's
Renwick Gallery (see p.209).

Two early Puerto Rican wood sculptures,
Santa Barbara from about 1680 to 1690 and
Nuestra Señora de los Dolores (Our Lady of Sorrows)
from about 1675 to 1725, are the oldest works in
the collection. Colonial America is represented
with portraits by John Singleton Copley,
Charles Willson Peale, and Gilbert Stuart,
landscapes by Thomas Cole, and sculptures by
Horatio Greenough.

For decades, the museum championed the
artists who captured the spirit of the frontier and
the lure of the West. George Catlin, Frederic
Remington, Thomas Moran, and Albert
Bierstadt celebrated the landscape and paid
tribute to Native Americans and their cultures.

The museum has one of the finest and largest
collections of American Impressionist paintings
and artwork from the last quarter of the 19th

ABOVE: The Luce Foundation
Center for American Art.

BELOW: Nam June Paik
(1932–2006). *Electronic
Superhighway: Continental
U.S., Alaska, Hawaii*, 1995.
51-channel video installation
(including one closed-circuit
television feed), custom
electronics, neon lighting,
steel, and wood; color,
sound. Gift of the artist.
© Nam June Paik Estate.

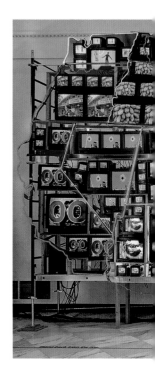

century, a period dubbed the "Gilded Age" by author Mark Twain. Artists included are Childe Hassam, Mary Cassatt, William Merritt Chase, Winslow Homer, John Singer Sargent, and James McNeill Whistler.

The country's largest collection of New Deal art and murals can also be found at the Smithsonian American Art Museum. Realist painters include Edward Hopper, John Sloan, and Andrew Wyeth.

Some American modernists, like Georgia O'Keeffe and Joseph Stella, captured the spirit of their age with inventive new ways of depicting the world, while artists such as Willem de Kooning and Franz Kline created wholly abstract compositions. Other important 20th-century painters in the collection are Marsden Hartley, Stuart Davis, Wayne Thiebaud, Alfred Jensen, and Philip Guston.

In recent years, the museum has focused on acquiring major works by modern and contemporary artists, including Oscar Bluemner, Christo, Nancy Graves, David Hockney, Jenny Holzer, Edward and Nancy Kienholz, Liz Larner, Roy Lichtenstein, Nam June Paik, Martin Puryear, and James Rosenquist.

ABOVE: William H. Johnson (1901–1970). *Café,* about 1939–40. Oil on paperboard. Gift of the Harmon Foundation.

The museum's sculpture collection, ranging from works by 19th-century masters Horatio Greenough, Harriet Hosmer, Edmonia Lewis, and Augustus Saint-Gaudens to renowned 20th-century artists Louise Nevelson, Isamu Noguchi, and Edward Kienholz, is the largest collection of American sculpture anywhere. Works on paper constitute a large part of the collection, notably prints from the 20th century and more than 150 years of photography.

The Smithsonian American Art Museum also has a long tradition of championing works that initially did not have a place in the story of American art. The museum was one of the first museums to collect and display folk and self-taught art in its galleries. In the last decade, it has acquired almost 500 pieces of Latino art, spanning colonial times to today.

LUNDER CONSERVATION CENTER

The Lunder Conservation Center is the first art conservation facility with floor-to-ceiling glass windows that allow the public permanent behind-the-scenes views of the museum's preservation work. Visitors can learn about conservation science through educational kiosks, videos, and public programs.

ROBERT AND ARLENE KOGOD COURTYARD

The Robert and Arlene Kogod Courtyard is enclosed with an elegant glass canopy, a signature element shared by the Smithsonian American Art Museum and the National Portrait Gallery. It was designed by world-renowned architects Foster + Partners and provides a distinctive, contemporary accent to the Greek Revival building.

LEFT: George Catlin (1796-1872). *Buffalo Bull's Back Fat, Head Chief, Blood Tribe,* 1832. Oil on canvas. Gift of Mrs. Joseph Harrison Jr.

OPPOSITE: Lily Furedi (1932-2006). *Subway,* 1934. Oil on canvas. Transfer from the US Department of the Interior, National Park Service.

GENERAL INFORMATION

INFORMATION DESK
Located in the lobby

TOURS
Walk-in tours are offered. For
information on group tours,
call 202-633-1000.

PUBLIC PROGRAMS
Free public programs include lectures,
gallery talks, films, family days, and
performances of music and dance.
For information call 202-633-1000 or
visit americanart.si.edu/events.

SHOPPING
The museum stores on the first floor
feature collection-inspired gifts, note
cards, posters, books, calendars,
jewelry, and more.

DINING
The Courtyard Café offers casual dining
with a seasonal menu of American
dishes. It is open from 11:30 a.m. to
4 p.m.; coffee, beer, and wine and light
fare are available until 6:30 p.m.

RENWICK GALLERY
OF THE SMITHSONIAN AMERICAN ART MUSEUM

Changing exhibitions of American crafts and decorative arts—historic and contemporary as well as selections from the permanent collection of 20th- and 21st-century American crafts—are on view in this historic structure. The building was the first purpose-built art museum in America, designed to showcase the art and cultural achievements of the still-new nation.

OPPOSITE: Leo Villareal (b. 1967). *Volume (Renwick)*, 2015. White LEDs, mirror-finished stainless steel, custom software, and electrical hardware. Gift of Janet and Jim Dicke, Tania and Tom Evans, Paula and Peter Lunder, and Debbie Petersen in honor of Elizabeth Broun. © Leo Villareal.

Pennsylvania Avenue at 17th Street NW

Open daily from 10 a.m. to 5:30 p.m. Closed December 25

Metrorail: Farragut West station (17th Street exit)

Smithsonian information: 202-633-1000

Museum information: 202-633-7970

americanart.si.edu

The Renwick Gallery, a branch of the Smithsonian American Art Museum, is dedicated to the future of art. It exhibits the most exciting works by American craft artists who are taking both traditional and innovative approaches to their materials and continually expanding the definitions of craft and art. The building, a national historic landmark named in honor of its architect, James Renwick Jr., has been home to the museum's contemporary craft program since 1972. The permanent collections galleries on the second floor emphasize a philosophy of craft as a way of living differently in the modern world through extraordinary handmade objects, while the first-floor galleries host special rotating exhibitions and installations. Artists whose works have been shown at the Renwick Gallery include Vivian Beer, Wendell Castle, Nick Cave, Dale Chihuly, Mary Jackson, Karen LaMonte, Albert Paley, Ken Price, Lenore Tawney, Peter Voulkos, and many others.

The gallery has always emphasized contemporary work, although special exhibitions sometimes feature historical traditions to trace the evolution of craft movements. The works on view showcase artists who have a genius for working with materials in inventive ways that transform our everyday world. The Rubenstein Grand Salon, a 4,300-square-foot gallery with a soaring 38-foot ceiling, is considered one of Washington's premier interior spaces.

OPPOSITE: Janet Echelman (b. 1966). *1.8 Renwick*, 2015. High-molecular-weight polyethylene, high-tenacity polyester, colored LED lighting, fans, control system, textile flooring, and textile filled with close-cell beads.

BELOW: Karen LaMonte (b. 1967). *Reclining Dress Impression with Drapery*, 2009. Glass. Gift of the James Renwick Alliance and Colleen and John Kotelly. © 2009, Karen LaMonte.

BUILDING HISTORY

The Renwick Gallery building was constructed in 1859 to house the art collection of William Wilson Corcoran, a prominent Washington philanthropist and banker. It was the first purpose-built art museum in America, a symbol of the nation's aspirations for distinctive cultural achievements. Corcoran engaged the noted architect James Renwick Jr., who had earlier designed the Smithsonian's Castle and St. Patrick's Cathedral in New York City. Renwick modeled the gallery in a French style that was first used in the pavilions of the Musée du Louvre, and he added distinctly American touches. When Corcoran's museum opened, it was considered one of the most elegant buildings in the country and hailed as the "American Louvre."

The building was dilapidated in the early 1960s and a proposal was made to tear it down, but First Lady Jackie Kennedy led the effort to save the architectural gem. In 1965, the gallery was turned over to the Smithsonian. Subsequently dedicated "for use as a gallery of art, crafts and design" and then extensively renovated, the Renwick building reopened in 1972 as the home of the Smithsonian American Art Museum's contemporary craft program. Four decades later, the Smithsonian American Art Museum again refurbished the Renwick Gallery to preserve its historical integrity and modernize it to meet the needs of a 21st-century museum. The Renwick reopened in November 2015 with a completely renewed infrastructure, enhanced historical features, upgraded technology, and a fresh, dynamic presentation of its permanent collection and new acquisitions.

OPPOSITE: Dale Chihuly (b. 1941). *Seafoam and Amber-Tipped Chandelier*, 1994. Glass and silver leaf. Gift of Barbaralee Diamonstein-Spielvogel. © 1994, Chihuly Studio.

BELOW: Wayne Higby (b. 1943). *Temple's Gates Pass*, 1988. Hand-built, raku-fired, and glazed earthenware. © 1988, Wayne Higby.

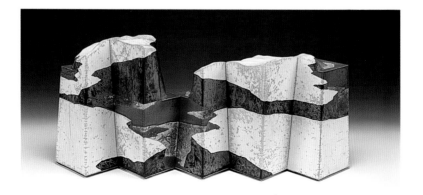

GENERAL INFORMATION

INFORMATION DESK
In the lobby

TOURS
Walk-in tours with museum docents
are offered. Group tours must be
arranged in advance by calling
202-633-8550.

PUBLIC PROGRAMS
Free public programs include craft
demonstrations, gallery talks, films,
and illustrated lectures. For
information, call 202-633-1000
or visit americanart.si.edu/events.

SHOPPING
The museum store features Renwick
publications and other craft and
decorative art books, craft objects
relating to exhibitions, postcards,
note cards, holiday cards, posters,
calendars, and jewelry.

ANACOSTIA COMMUNITY MUSEUM

The Anacostia Community Museum was established in 1967 as the nation's first federally funded neighborhood museum. It has evolved into a significant national resource focused on issues of contemporary urban life as an outgrowth of its earlier African American history mission. With this foundation, research, exhibitions, collections, and public programs have expanded.

OPPOSITE: Fan quilt, late 19th to early 20th century. Silk, velvet, corduroy blocks set on point.

1901 Fort Place SE

Open daily for onsite visits from noon to 5 p.m.; Tuesdays until 8 p.m. Closed December 25.

Metrorail: Anacostia station

Smithsonian information: 202-633-1000

Museum information: 202-633-4820

Check online for museum access updates: anacostia.si.edu

The Anacostia Community Museum enhances the understanding of contemporary urban life through its innovative community-based approach to research, exhibitions, and public programming. Building upon more than five decades of work in history and culture, the museum explores and documents how people engage, shape, respond to, and confront contemporary issues. The museum addresses universal themes of empowerment, neighborhood change, racial inequality, and globalization through an examination of community history and cultural traditions; growth and economic and environmental realities; and interaction between diverse communities and the arts.

Scholars and researchers find compelling opportunities to use the excellent research facilities at the Anacostia Community Museum. The collection reflects neighborhood and city history, women's history, literature, family history, and African American studies. Archival materials, photographs, artwork, and artifacts can be viewed on the museum's website and are available to the public through remote and in-person research appointments. Museum research examines concerns such as urban ecology, neighborhood change, and cultural encounters and initiates documentation projects to record the history and changes in the local urban community. This work is the basis for exploring local issues with national resonance that are addressed in exhibitions and associated activities presented in the gallery, online or offsite, under the museums expanded direction. Just as the research, collection development, and outreach are models for replication by other community-oriented museums, so are the museum's public programs. Through the varied streaming and/or onsite programs held annually, the museum offers further interpretation of exhibitions on view and online, expands on research and collections topics, and presents music and other performance-based youth and family programs.

TOP: Chuck Brown (1936–2012), the "Godfather of Go Go" owned this guitar. Created by local musicians in Southeast Washington, DC, Go Go has been designated the official music of the District of Columbia by the mayor and city council.

LEFT: A native of Southwest DC and International Boxing Hall of Fame boxer Mark "Too Sharp" Johnson donated this pair of custom-made boxing shoes.

OPPOSITE: "I am honored to have witnessed and captured such a monumental moment in history," noted Alexandria, VA, resident Talia Hawley in her story about her church's June 2020 Black Lives Matter march to DC. She donated it to ACM's Moments of Resilience online initiative featuring stories of support regarding COVID-19 and the social justice movement. Photo by Talia Hawley.

GENERAL INFORMATION

HOW TO GET THERE
The Anacostia Community Museum is located in historic Fort Stanton Park in Southeast Washington, DC, with ample parking for cars and buses.

By Metrorail and Metrobus: Take the Green Line to the Anacostia station and transfer to the W-2 or W-3 Metrobus to the museum.

By car: From downtown, take the Southeast Freeway (I-395) to the 11th Street Bridge and exit onto Martin Luther King Jr. Avenue. At the fourth traffic light, turn left at Morris Road and drive up the hill to the museum on the right. From 1-295 south: Take the Howard Road exit and turn left on Howard Road. Travel to Martin Luther King Jr. Avenue and turn left. Turn right at Morris Road and continue up the hill to the museum.

ACCESSIBILITY
The facility is wheelchair accessible, with ramps off the parking lot near all entrances, automatic opening entry doors, and handicap-designated parking spaces. All public spaces within the museum are wheelchair accessible.

PUBLIC PROGRAMS AND TOURS
Activities for adults, families, and youth include lectures, workshops, films, exhibitions, and performances on weekdays and weekends held virtually and onsite in the museum's renovated interior and exterior spaces. Extended onsite visitation hours are on Tuesdays until 8 p.m. for those unable to attend the museum during its regular hours of operation. The museum's robust website at anacostia.si.edu allows visitors to access virtual exhibitions, online educational resources, and event calendars with information on available streaming and/or onsite programming. To learn more about museum programs and exhibitions, visit anacostia.si.edu and subscribe to the e-calendar. While self-guided tours are encouraged for onsite visits, the website is the best source of up-to-date information on the availability of guided and virtual tours or call 202-633-4844. Follow the museum on Facebook, Twitter, and Instagram.

RESEARCH
The museum's research department provides remote and in-person fellowship and internship opportunities to undergraduate and graduate students in public history, community-oriented studies, urban waterways and environment, and African American studies. Internships are also available remotely or onsite in the collections, education, special events, public affairs, and marketing departments. For more information about internships and fellowships, call 202-633-4868 or email ACMinfo@si.edu.

NATIONAL ZOO

The Smithsonian's National Zoo and Conservation Biology Institute is always free of charge to enter and open 364 days per year. Founded in 1889, the Zoo sits on 163 acres in the heart of Rock Creek Park in Washington, DC, and is home to 2,700 animals representing more than 390 species. Visitors can see giant pandas, elephants, American bison, flamingos, cheetahs, tigers, seals, Panamanian gold frogs, and more.

OPPOSITE: The National Zoo is a leader in giant panda conservation.

Entrances: Connecticut Avenue NW (3001 block between Cathedral Avenue and Devonshire Place); Harvard Street and Adams Mill Road intersection; Beach Drive in Rock Creek Park

Open daily. Closed December 25.

Metrorail: Woodley Park/Zoo/Adams Morgan station or Cleveland Park station

Recorded information and Information Desk: 202-633-4888

nationalzoo.si.edu

The Smithsonian's National Zoo and Conservation Biology Institute is known internationally for the exhibiting, breeding, and study of wild animals. The Zoo instills a lifelong commitment to conservation through engaging experiences with animals and the people working to save them.

Vertebrate species, representing the most spectacular and familiar forms of land animals, make up the most visible part of the collection, but invertebrate and aquatic species provide a more comprehensive picture of animal life. Educational graphics and demonstrations, including animal training and enrichment, feeding, and keeper talks, supplement public understanding of the park's animals and plants.

Native and ornamental plants grow throughout the 163-acre park. The Zoo in Your Backyard (featuring plants that attract butterflies) provides living examples of the interaction among plants, animals, and humans. Olmsted Walk, the central path, connects the major animal exhibits. It is named for the father of landscape architecture, Frederick Law Olmsted, who created the original design for the National Zoo as well as the US Capitol grounds, the Washington National Cathedral grounds, and New York's Central Park.

EXHIBITS

The giant pandas occupy the top spot on the Zoo's "must see" list. The pandas' state-of-the-art habitat is designed to mimic their natural habitat of rocky, lush terrain in China. Each element has a purpose—from helping the pandas stay cool in hot weather to giving them a place to hide when they need privacy. Rock and tree structures are perfect for climbing, and grottoes, pools, and streams for keeping cool.

LEFT: The Smithsonian Conservation Biology Institute breeds Guam kingfishers, one of the world's rarest birds.

OPPOSITE: The Zoo's flamingos are a highlight for Bird House visitors.

The pandas are the gateway to the Asia Trail—nearly six acres of exhibits featuring endangered or threatened Asian species. Joining giant pandas along the Trail are clouded leopards, fishing cats, Asian small-clawed otters, red pandas, and sloth bears.

Along the American Trail, guests can wander through landscaped paths and discover unparalleled opportunities to come face-to-face with California sea lions and gray seals, watch playful beavers and otters, admire the classic beauty of eagles and wolves, and meet intelligent ravens. The American Trail showcases species that are gems of North American wildlife and treasures to us all. The animals here represent the triumph of the American spirit and success stories in conservation.

Asian elephants are critically endangered; fewer than 50,000 remain in their native countries. The National Zoo is committed to their conservation and to the powerful connection made when visitors experience the magnificence of elephants in the Zoo.

At Elephant Trails, visitors experience the sights, sounds, and smells of being close to the Zoo's Asian elephants. In addition, interactive exhibits teach visitors about elephants' physical characteristics, social behaviors, and intelligence and the commitment necessary to care for them at the Zoo.

The Elephant Trails exhibit spans 8,943 square meters, large enough to accommodate up to three separate groups of elephants, including a natural herd and individual bulls. Altogether, the facility can house between eight and ten adult Asian elephants and their young.

OPPOSITE: Giant pandas explore, play, eat, and sleep in their naturalistic habitat.

BELOW: Built on decades of science, the Zoo's Asian elephant conservation program is centered around caring for and studying this charismatic species.

TOP: The world's largest lizard, the Komodo dragon, uses its tongue to explore its environment.

ABOVE: Brilliantly colored green tree pythons are a favorite in the Zoo's Reptile Discovery Center.

RIGHT: The National Zoo's Golden Lion Tamarin Conservation Program has been heralded as the world's most successful primate conservation program. Visitors can see these monkeys inside year-round at the Small Mammal House.

The Reptile Discovery Center celebrates the diversity, beauty, and unique adaptations of more than 70 reptiles and amphibians—from giant crocodiles and tortoises, to stunning snakes and lizards, to colorful frogs and salamanders. Visitors can meet Cuban crocodiles, Aldabra tortoises, and Komodo dragons as they tour the historic building and surrounding grounds. At the Jewels of Appalachia exhibit, peer into the underground world of salamanders and learn about how these tiny creatures are critical to an entire ecosystem, as well as what Zoo scientists are doing to save them.

In the Small Mammal House, come face to face with the sprightly grace of the golden lion tamarin, the uncanny armor of the three-banded armadillo, and the fascinating quills of the prehensile-tailed porcupine. Gaze at naked mole rats as they move from chamber to chamber, and observe the tamandua—an arboreal anteater—searching in logs for its favorite treats: mealworms. Catch a glimpse of rare animals that were on the verge of extinction, like the black-footed ferret, or see something native to your own backyard, such as the striped skunk.

Think Tank introduces visitors to the science of animal cognition. Thinking ability in animals is presented through the topics of tool use, language, and society. Orangutans, hermit crabs, Norway rats—as well as their computers and games—stimulate exploration. Orangutans can move between the Think Tank and their Great Ape House enclosures, several hundred feet farther along Olmsted Walk, by swinging, or brachiating, across the O-Line. This series of towers connected by heavy cables allows orangutans to move as they would in their heavily forested, tropical homes.

ABOVE: Several of the National Zoo's orangutans participate in a computer-based language project at Think Tank.

LEFT: The National Zoo's gorilla family gives visitors insights into the great ape's behavior and social structure.

Great Cats is home territory for some of the visitors' favorite animals: lions and tigers.

A walk through Amazonia introduces visitors to the high degree of biological diversity in a tropical rain forest. The 15,000-square-foot rain forest habitat of the exhibit includes a 55,000-gallon aquarium for the display of Amazon River fish. Within Amazonia's dome, visitors find a living tropical forest with more than 350 species of plants, including 50-foot-tall trees, tropical vines, and epiphytes. This habitat is also home to species of mammals, birds, and insects typical of the Amazon Basin, all moving throughout the exhibit.

The Amazonia Science Gallery is an 8,000-square-foot experimental science education/outreach center that brings visitors into the day-to-day world of scientific research and the people who do it. The gallery includes Amphibian Alert! featuring more than fifteen species of frogs and other amphibians, including the extinct-in-the-wild Panamanian golden frog. Through close-up animal views visitors discover what's threatening these amphibian "jewels" and what's being done to save them. At the Coral Lab exhibit, watch the tentacles of the elegance coral sway in the current and spot clownfish hiding among the anemones. Learn how Zoo scientists have pioneered techniques for collecting and freezing the genetic material of more than a dozen coral species.

The Visitor Center, near the Connecticut Avenue entrance, has an auditorium, souvenir shop, and restrooms.

TOP: The National Zoo's Cheetah Conservation Station allows visitors to see this endangered cat in a naturalistic habitat that encourages behavior typical to that observed in the wild.

ABOVE: Scimitar-horned oryx can be seen in the Zoo's Cheetah Conservation Station.

BELOW: Tigers, extremely rare in the wild, are ambassadors for the Zoo's conservation and science initiatives.

CONSERVATION AND RESEARCH

What the visitor sees at the National Zoo reveals only a small part of the Zoo's complexity as a scientific research organization. National Zoo scientists, working on the grounds in Washington, DC, and at the 3,200-acre Smithsonian Conservation Biology Institute in Front Royal, Virginia, were among the founders of the field of conservation biology. National Zoo scientists continue as leaders today, with global perspectives and long-term experience in conducting zoo and field-based research. Their discoveries enhance the survival or recovery of species and their habitats, helping to ensure the health and well-being of animals in zoos and their counterparts in the wild. The National Zoo is also a global leader in training the next generation of conservation and zoo professionals, through undergraduate, graduate, and professional education that emphasizes well-founded approaches to conservation.

HISTORY

Although the Smithsonian Institution received gifts of live animals almost from its beginning, it had no zoo to house and study the living collection. Some of the animals were sent to zoos elsewhere; some were kept on the National Mall. Over the years, a sizable menagerie accumulated outside the Smithsonian Castle. In 1889, Congress established the National Zoological Park at the urging of Samuel Pierpont Langley, third secretary of the Smithsonian, and William T. Hornaday, a Smithsonian naturalist who was particularly

ABOVE: A male Panamanian gold frog at the National Zoo is part of a Species Survival Plan.

concerned about the looming extinction of the American bison. Six bison were among the animals transferred from the Mall to the National Zoo when the grounds opened in 1891.

Animal collecting expeditions in the early 1900s, together with gifts from individuals and foreign governments and exchanges with other zoos, augmented the Zoo's population and introduced Washingtonians to rare and exotic animals, including the Tasmanian wolf (now extinct), bongo, and Komodo dragon.

Today, the National Zoo continues to develop a bond between humans and animals that helps visitors understand biology and scientific concepts that will guide them in making informed choices in daily life. Exhibits, educational programs, school programs, training opportunities, and public lectures all bring the rich diversity of life on Earth to local, national, and international audiences. In the 21st century, the Zoo's mission is to provide leadership in animal care science, conservation, and public education.

LEFT: In 1887, William T. Hornaday—chief taxidermist for the Smithsonian—proposed that Congress establish a National Zoo after seeing the bison population decline. On March 2, 1889, Congress passed an act establishing the National Zoological Park. The Zoo officially became a part of the Smithsonian in 1890 and opened to the public on April 30, 1891, in its current Rock Creek Park location.

BELOW: In winter 2022, the Zoo's historic 1928 Bird House will transform into a first-of-its-kind attraction that immerses visitors in the annual journeys of Western Hemisphere birds, including sanderlings.

OPPOSITE: Sunbathing seals attract visitors to the Zoo's American Trail.

GENERAL INFORMATION

HOW TO GET THERE
The Zoo is accessible from the Woodley Park/Zoo/Adams Morgan and Cleveland Park Metrorail stations and by Metrobus. For Metro information, call 202-637-7000 or check the website wmata.com. Limited pay parking is available on Zoo lots. Bus-passenger discharge and pickup and limited free bus parking are available. Pickup and drop-off locations are also available for visitors using a ride-share service.

HOURS (UNLESS POSTED OTHERWISE)
March 15–September 30: Animal exhibits are open from 9 a.m. to 6 p.m. every day. October 1–March 14: Animal exhibits are open from 9 a.m. to 4 p.m. every day. The Zoo is open every day except December 25.

ACCESSIBILITY
The Zoo has ramped building entrances and restroom facilities for visitors with disabilities. Strollers may be rented in season for a small fee. A limited number of wheelchairs are available to rent. Zoo police provide lost-and-found service and a refuge for lost children.

DINING
The Zoo has various dining facilities. Picnic areas are located throughout the grounds, but no outdoor cooking is permitted.

SHOPPING
Unique zoo-oriented souvenirs, toys, postcards, books, T-shirts, and jewelry are for sale.

FEEDING TIMES
Visit the Zoo's website for animal encounters, feeding, and demonstration times. nationalzoo.si.edu/visit/daily-events

MEMBERSHIP
A Smithsonian's National Zoo Membership will send you on a fun-filled journey with exclusive experiences and discounts on parking, shopping, dining, and more. Your membership supports animal conservation and wildlife research. To learn more, visit nationalzoo.si.edu/membership.

HELPFUL HINTS
Consider using public transportation. Zoo parking lots often fill up early. Wear comfortable clothing and shoes. Fall and early winter are great times to visit the Zoo. Learn more about the Zoo's animals and conservation efforts through entertaining and educational videos, available online at nationalzoo.si.edu.

SOME RULES TO FOLLOW
Pets, except certified assistance animals, are not permitted in the park. The area between the guardrail and the enclosure barrier is for your safety and that of the animals. Stay on your side of the guardrail. Zoo animals are wild and easily excited. Do not feed or attempt to touch the animals. The Zoo provides excellent, balanced diets, and additional feeding is unhealthy for them. Do not skate or ride bicycles in the park. Radios and other audio devices must be used with headphones.

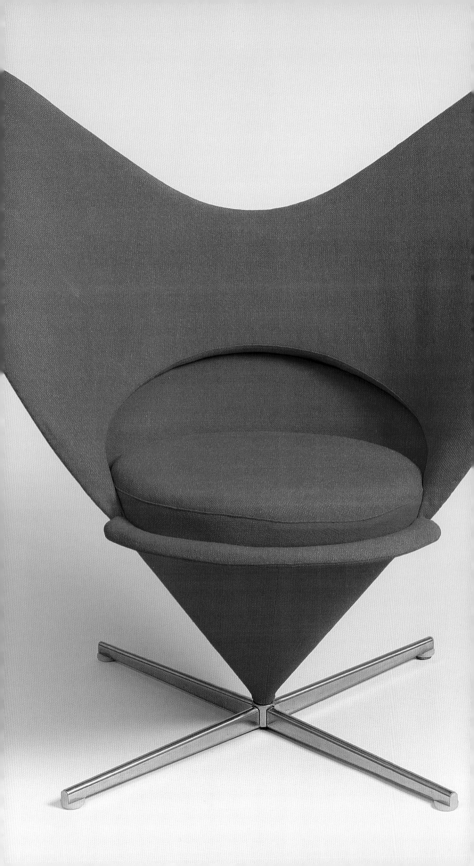

COOPER HEWITT,
SMITHSONIAN
DESIGN MUSEUM

Cooper Hewitt is America's design museum. Inclusive, innovative, and experimental, the museum's dynamic exhibitions, education programs, master's program, publications, and online resources inspire, educate, and empower people through design.

OPPOSITE: Verner Panton (1926–1998). Heart cone chair, 1959. Steel, stainless steel, molded plastic, woven wool upholstery. Gift of George R. Kravis II (2018-22-57).

2 East 91st Street (at Fifth Avenue), New York City

Open daily, 10 a.m. to 6 p.m.; Tuesdays, 10 a.m. to 8 p.m. Closed Thanksgiving and December 25.

Admission fee; Pay What You Wish, Tuesdays, 6 p.m. to 8 p.m.

212-849-8400

cooperhewitt.org

ABOUT THE MUSEUM

Steward of one of the world's most diverse and comprehensive design collections—over 210,000 objects that range from an ancient Egyptian faience cup dating to about 1100 BCE to contemporary 3D-printed objects and digital code—Cooper Hewitt welcomes everyone to discover the importance of design and its power to change the world.

Cooper Hewitt is located on New York City's Museum Mile in the historic, landmark Carnegie Mansion. The grounds include the Arthur Ross Terrace and Garden, the city's largest private garden.

Founded in 1897, Cooper Hewitt is the only museum in the nation devoted exclusively to historic and contemporary design. In 2014, Cooper Hewitt reopened in the renovated and restored Andrew Carnegie Mansion with 60 percent more exhibition space than it previously had and a completely reimagined visitor experience. Interactive galleries throughout the museum's four floors now encourage visitors to explore the collection digitally on ultra-high-definition touch-screen tables and draw their own designs in the Immersion Room.

Technology is a key element of the reinvigorated museum, which has been a branch of the Smithsonian since 1967.

EXHIBITIONS

Cooper Hewitt's galleries present temporary exhibitions as well as installations drawn from the permanent collection.

On the first floor are the Process Galleries, Process Lab, and the Nancy and Edwin Marks Gallery, which provide an exciting introduction to design from many time periods.

LEFT: Louis Comfort Tiffany (1848–1933). Peacock vase, ca. 1901. Produced by Tiffany Glass and Decorating Company (New York, New York, USA). Mold-blown favrile glass. Gift of Stanley Siegel, from the Stanley Siegel Collection (1975-32-11).

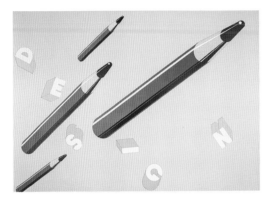

The entire second floor is dedicated to showcasing objects from the museum's permanent collection and features exhibitions that juxtapose the historic and the contemporary. Here, the Models & Prototypes Gallery provides insights into the important role of architectural models and design prototypes in the design process. Featured objects have included 18th- and 19th-century staircase models and 19th-century botanical models and illustrated books. The former Carnegie Family Library on the second floor displays intricately ornamental teak woodwork created by Lockwood de Forest.

The open-plan Barbara and Morton Mandel Design Gallery on the third floor hosts major special exhibitions. Ranging from broad surveys on contemporary design to compelling retrospectives on design legends, Cooper Hewitt's rotating exhibitions serve as inspiration for creative work of all kinds and tell the story of design's paramount importance in improving our world.

LEFT: Takenobu Igarashi (b. 1944). Poster, *Identity*, 1976. Lithograph on paper. Gift of Takenobu Igarashi (2018-18-5).

BELOW: *Botanical Expressions* features interpretations of botanical form through decorative arts of the late 18th through the early 20th centuries.

DESIGN TRIENNIAL

Cooper Hewitt's renowned *Triennial* exhibition series was launched in 2000 to critical acclaim. The only exhibition of its kind in the country, it showcases some of the most exciting, provocative, and innovative design created around the globe during the previous three years. The *Triennial* presents work from emerging talent and established designers in the fields of fashion, architecture, graphics, digital media, and furniture.

COLLECTIONS

Cooper Hewitt's four curatorial departments (Drawings, Prints, and Graphic Design; Product Design and Decorative Arts; Textiles; and Wallcoverings) oversee one of the most diverse design collections in existence: more than 210,000 objects that span 30 centuries. The core collection was formed between the late 19th and early 20th centuries by the museum's founders, Sarah and Eleanor Hewitt, who conceived it as a "practical working laboratory," a "visual library" where students and designers could be inspired by actual objects. In addition to furniture, metalwork, glass, ceramics, jewelry, woodwork, textiles, and wallcoverings, the museum has one of the largest collections of drawings and prints in the United States, spanning the fields of architecture, advertising, fashion, fine art, theater, and interior design. The mission of the collection has always been to highlight history, innovation, process,

OPPOSITE: Jacquemart & Benard (Paris, France). *La Chasse au Faucon (Falcon Hunt)*, Sidewall, 1794–1797. Block-printed on handmade paper. Gift of Eleanor and Sarah Hewitt (1931-45-28).

LEFT: Alexandra Agudelo (b. 1965). Mollo bowl (Colombia), 2018. Silver, gold. Gift of the artist and Cristina Grajales (2019-6-1).

BELOW: Gilles-Marie Oppenord (1672–1742). Drawing, Preliminary Design for the Salon d'Angle at the Palais Royal, Paris, France, 1719-20. Purchased for the Museum by the Advisory Council (1911-28-80).

technique, use, aesthetics, and social context. The current collecting priorities include representing designers from diverse communities, reflecting the museums commitment to sustainable and socially responsible design, expanding digital and cross–disciplinary design collecting, and shaping the collection through scholarship.

TOP: Alexander Hayden Girard (1907–1993). Triangles textile, 1952. Manufactured by Herman Miller Textiles (Zeeland, Michigan, USA). Screen-printed linen. Gift of George R. Kravis II (2016-5-28).

BELOW: J. (Jean) Persoz (1805–1868). *Traité théorique et pratique de l'impression des tissus // par J. Persoz*, 4 v. : diagrs., patterns. Atlas (20 leaves of plates : ill. (partly double, partly col.). Smithsonian Libraries.

OPPOSITE: Ilonka Karasz (1896–1981). Calico cow textile, 1952. Cotton textile American Textile History Museum Collection. Gift of Michele Palmer (2017-24-7).

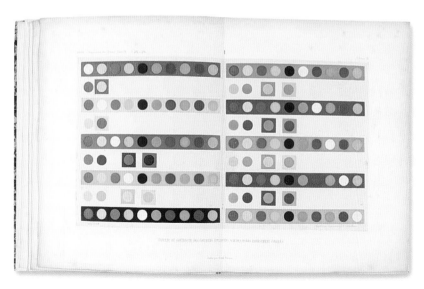

GENERAL INFORMATION

VISITOR SERVICES
Just inside the main entrance

TOURS
Private and self-guided tours for groups of 10 or more are available by reservation at 212-849-8351; public tours, offered twice daily, are free with admission.

SHOPPING
The SHOP features significant design objects from around the world and focuses on American designers. Offerings reflect the museum's design philosophy, mission, and collection and include items related to current exhibitions.

DINING
Cooper Hewitt's café offers a seasonal menu and a variety of coffees, pastries, and artisanal wines. Seating is available indoors and outdoors in the adjoining Arthur Ross Terrace and Garden. Like the garden, the café is open to the public, free of charge, beginning at 8 a.m. weekdays.

EDUCATIONAL PROGRAMS
Cooper Hewitt's extensive education programs include activities for all ages, from public lectures to hands-on workshops. Design Field Trips bring students into the museum to explore current exhibitions and participate in a workshop. In association with Parsons School of Design, the museum also offers an on-site master's program in the history of design and curatorial studies.

SMITHSONIAN DESIGN LIBRARY
The Smithsonian Design Library's 90,000 volumes—including 10,000 rare books on ornament, architecture, and decorative arts—is an unparalleled resource for design and decorative arts materials from the Renaissance to the present. The library is open by appointment.

SUPPORT THE SMITHSONIAN

YOUR CONTRIBUTIONS MATTER

As the world's largest museum and research and educational complex, the Smithsonian tells America's story. While our facilities and core operations are supported through federal funding, private philanthropic support is needed to fund efforts to bring the Smithsonian's vast collections, scholarship, and research to millions of people around the world. The generosity of donors helps to fulfill that need, strengthening the Smithsonian and supporting the work of its talented curators, scholars, scientists, and educators.

There are many ways you can contribute to the Smithsonian. Donors may make outright gifts to be used where they are most needed or designate their gifts to a particular museum, research institute, or special program. Gifts may be made in honor or memory of another person. In addition to monetary gifts, the Smithsonian also accepts gifts of stock, distributions from retirement accounts, and contributions from donor advised funds. Some gifts may qualify to be matched by an employer.

Membership giving is one of the easiest ways to support the Smithsonian, allowing individuals to join together to create the greatest philanthropic impact. Membership programs, including the *Friends of the Smithsonian*, *National Associates*, and *Smithsonian Associates*, offer rewarding benefits at a variety of levels in addition to providing invaluable resources for the Smithsonian. For donors interested in more targeted giving, some Smithsonian museums offer their own membership programs.

Including the Smithsonian in an individual's estate plans is a way to help our museums and research centers to remain vital places of learning and discovery for future generations. Some of the most popular ways to create a legacy at the Smithsonian include giving through a will or trust, establishing charitable gift annuities, or naming the Smithsonian as a beneficiary in retirement accounts, life insurance policies, and other assets. The Smithsonian Legacy Society recognizes the commitment and generosity of these donors.

More in-depth information about all of these philanthropic activities can be found on the Smithsonian website, si.edu, or by calling 1-800-931-3226.

SMITHSONIAN MEMBERSHIPS

By joining one or more of our membership groups, individuals can deepen their relationship with the Smithsonian and help shape the future by preserving America's heritage, discovering new knowledge, and sharing this nation's resources with the world.

FRIENDS OF THE SMITHSONIAN

Friends of the Smithsonian play a pivotal role in every Smithsonian experience. Members provide significant philanthropic support to present our exhibitions, which represent the nation's rich heritage, art from across the globe, and immense diversity of the natural and cultural world. This membership support also provides educational resources that ignite a passion for learning and discovery.

Friends who give $75–$999 receive a wide variety of benefits, such as:
*   Smithsonian annual engagement calendar
*   Subscription to *Smithsonian Magazine*
*   Recognition in the Friends of the Smithsonian Honor Roll
*   Free admission to the Cooper Hewitt, Smithsonian Design Museum
*   20 percent discount at Smithsonian Museum Stores, 10 percent discount to select dining facilities and the Smithsonian catalog, member rate for Smithsonian theaters
*   Smithsonian museum guidebooks and exhibit publications
*   Special events throughout the year at Smithsonian museums

The Castle Circle is a leadership level group within the Friends that exemplifies the spirit of giving. Members give $1,000–$2,499 annually and receive benefits including:
*   Special invitations to members-only tours, receptions, and lectures
*   Invitation to an exclusive Castle Circle reception in a museum after-hours
*   Newsletters with insider information
*   All other Friends of the Smithsonian benefits

Membership in the James Smithson Society, where annual gifts start at $2,500, builds on the legacy of the Smithsonian's founding donor. The philanthropic leadership of this dedicated group ensures the Institution remains a vibrant place of discovery. Among the Society's specially designed benefits are:
*   Invitation for two to the Annual Smithsonian Weekend
*   Private receptions and early entry at select Friends of the Smithsonian events
*   Invitation to an exclusive James Smithson Society exhibition opening or behind-the-scenes tours
*   Special recognition in the Smithsonian annual report and other publications
*   All other Castle Circle and Friends of the Smithsonian benefits

For more information, call 800-931-3226 or visit SmithsonianMembership.org.

SMITHSONIAN ENTERPRISES

Smithsonian Enterprises supports the Smithsonian through commercial activities, including media memberships. The proceeds from these activities support Smithsonian research, administration, and programming.

When you visit us at the Smithsonian, you can help support the institution by shopping in our museum stores, dining at our restaurants and cafés, and watching a movie in our IMAX® theaters. At home, visit www.smithsonian.com to continue your support. You can subscribe to our magazines and e-newsletters, sign up for the Smithsonian Channel, purchase toys, jewelry, and collectables from the Smithsonian, buy Smithsonian published books, and travel with Smithsonian Journeys.

NATIONAL ASSOCIATES

This membership is open to all members nationwide and worldwide, and offers benefits, including:

- Subscription to *Smithsonian Magazine* (11 issues)
- Free admission to the Cooper Hewitt, Smithsonian Design Museum
- Discounts to select Smithsonian dining facilities, theaters, and other services
- Exclusive member discount on The Great Courses, including topics such as history, science, better living, and travel
- 10 percent member discount on Smithsonian Folkways Recordings purchased at folkways.si.edu
- Purchase limited-edition art at member discounts through the Smithsonian Associates Art Collectors Program

SMITHSONIAN ASSOCIATES

This membership program offers Washington-area residents and anyone visiting the nation's capital an array of lectures, classes, and special events. Members are part of the largest museum-based cultural and educational program in the world and have special access to the Smithsonian's resources. Membership directly supports Smithsonian Associate programming and outreach efforts. Among the benefits of membership are:

- Subscription to the monthly Smithsonian Associates program guide
- Savings on more than 750 educational and cultural programs
- Member-only events
- Discounts at Smithsonian museum stores, SmithsonainStore.com, select dining facilities, and the Smithsonian Catalog

For more information, call 202-633-3030 or visit SmithsonianAssociates.org.

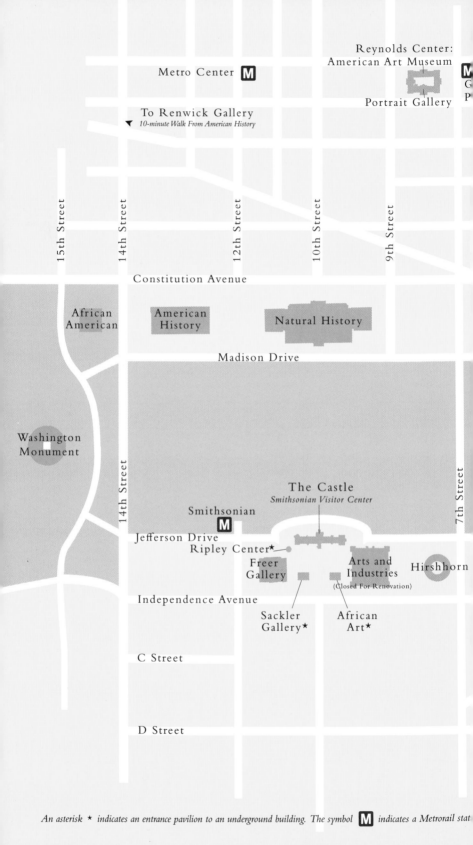

Reynolds Center:
American Art Museum

Metro Center **M**

Portrait Gallery

M
G
P

To Renwick Gallery
▼ *10-minute Walk From American History*

15th Street

14th Street

12th Street

10th Street

9th Street

Constitution Avenue

African
American

American
History

Natural History

Madison Drive

Washington
Monument

14th Street

The Castle
Smithsonian Visitor Center

Smithsonian
M

7th Street

Jefferson Drive

Ripley Center★

Freer
Gallery

Arts and
Industries
(Closed For Renovation)

Hirshhorn

Independence Avenue

Sackler
Gallery★

African
Art★

C Street

D Street

An asterisk ★ indicates an entrance pavilion to an underground building. The symbol **M** *indicates a Metrorail stat*